Y0-BUD-531

4-16-74

Elsie Lee's
Party
Cookbook

ALSO BY ELSIE LEE

NONFICTION:

Elsie Lee's Book of Simple Gourmet Cookery
The Bachelor's Cookbook
Easy Gourmet Cooking
The Second Easy Gourmet Cookbook

FICTION:

Prior Betrothal
The Passions of Medora Graeme
Wingarden

Elsie Lee's Party Cookbook

ARBOR HOUSE

NEW YORK

THIS BOOK IS GRATEFULLY DEDICATED
TO
MURRAY AND BEN
HAROLD AND MORRIS
ROSE HIMMELSTEIN
WITHOUT WHOM I COULD NEVER
ADEQUATELY TEST **ANY** RECIPES

Contents

Introduction

The success of *Elsie Lee's Book of Simple Gourmet Cookery* naturally demands a follow-up. Any woman knows that if one of something is good, two will be better.

The original collection of recipes was intended for family use, although many were fancy enough for guests. However, I deliberately omitted all the dishes I serve for entertaining, principally because the SGC was quite long enough to begin with. I went rather thoroughly into basics of equipment, spices, and cooking methods. There was a section on shopping addresses for uncommon ingredients, and another on using up leftovers of egg whites or tomato paste. It was a very comprehensive book, if I do say so, but this now creates a major dilemma.

It seems unfair to repeat any of my words of wisdom, if you already own *Simple Gourmet Cookery*. Neither do I wish to give the impression that you can't use my *Party Cookbook* except teamed with SGC, because of course you can. Still, if you don't have it, will you know what *I* mean by "flambé" or "thicken with egg yolks?" After long communing with my soul, I am repeating those six pages on Methods, mostly to avoid lengthy repetitive instructions in individual recipes. Otherwise this book is entirely distinct from *Simple Gourmet Cookery*.

These recipes are meant for *entertaining*: everything from two to twenty or more people. No one of these appears in *Simple Gourmet Cookery*, and as before, they are meant for the woman who has graduated from Fanny and Irma, but is not quite ready for *Gourmet*, volumes I and II. There is nothing here that requires either a large staff or an unlimited bank account—everything can be prepared alone and unaided, although it is nice to have someone to clean up when you're finished.

In the following pages you will find a dissertation on party-giving, the basics of planning the menu and scheduling preparation work, plus recipes as accurate and explicit as I can make them. Some are designed for the woman delayed at the office with four guests expected—others are for the woman who will have all day at home, but also has babies to be fed, bathed and bedded before party time. When I lived in Washington, I was forever expecting old friends motoring through, and heaven knew when they'd arrive, depending on traffic or weather conditions. What was needed was food that improved by waiting or reheating. Now that I'm back in New York, I am annually importuned to contribute to the Block Party, which is the urban equivalent of a country Community House supper.

There are recipes to cover all such eventualities, as well as a few for Christmas presents.

I am giving some sample menus, but you must learn to make your own. These are only a guide for how-to-do-it. Cuddled among the hundred and three cookbooks that crowd my shelves are a number on menus, but I have never yet found one that *I* would follow without a change. A menu is a personal thing. It should be what you like to prepare, what your guests will like to eat . . . and I don't know your guests.

These are only what I serve my friends, so you will find gaps. I live in the city, and my parties are primarily in the evening. It is different in suburbia or the real country, where you can have a tailgate picnic before the races or a buffet lunch for the Ladies' Aid sewing circle. In my youth I was well acquainted with such things, even debutante teas (do they still exist?) and "refreshments" after the bridge party. I bet I made as many cakes, pies and salads as any of you when the neighbors in our summer village would meet in the Community House.

I no longer live that sort of life, hence my parties are primarily late afternoon through evening. Similarly the menus are geared for that period. This doesn't mean you won't find anything usable for breakfast and luncheon—I have included recipes for every kind of entertaining. Unfortunately, the basic rule of "never serve a guest a dish you haven't tried first" cannot apply to parties. How are you to *try* Bollito Misto until you have a dozen people to eat it up? Occasionally one must cross everything from eyes down to toes, and plunge!

On the strict understanding that you will do EXACTLY what I tell you in a large-scale recipe, I will guarantee an edible result—but you must *read* the directions all the way through. Do not blithely embark on something with simple ingredients only to discover it must be chilled overnight or takes three hours to bake after ten minutes of stirring it together!

This is a book of fairly easy recipes intended to create a major effect—but you must still use your head a little bit. Many recipes can be halved for fewer people—or doubled, even tripled, for a crowd. You may need an extra pound of meat or chicken, if your guests are hearty eaters . . . and it is manifestly absurd to use spices or herbs nobody likes. Perhaps they can be omitted without damage to the end product? Or perhaps you are clever enough to be able to substitute another flavoring for what you omitted? By now you should certainly know enough to note in the margin what alterations you made!

Otherwise you're on your own. *Bon appétit!*

I Believe...

Too few people understand the meaning of gourmet food or cookery. It is not rich, expensive, fussy to prepare, nor does it require hard-to-get components. What it *is* is food that is good to eat because it is seasoned to your taste, cooked to the exact degree of doneness you prefer, and there is just enough of it to provide gentle fullness of the tummy without burps. Oddly enough, a great many people in our country have always eaten this way. We just never knew it was gourmet.

Food somehow tastes better when it has a name. Make it up for yourself, relying heavily on what you know of foreign gastronomic names. If the seasonings are oregano-garlic-tomato, it is à l'Italienne, if they are curry-coriander-soy sauce, it is Orientale, and so on. When in doubt, anything can be billed as *Chez Vous* or *à la Maison*.

No dinner table should be constructed to seat more than eight people who are not blood relatives! If it's essential to seat ten, twelve or more (although who has that big a dining room these days?), the central flower arrangement MUST be tall enough to prevent any cross-table conversation. Otherwise the place will sound like a flock of peahens, and you will be so distracted you'll forget to serve the casserole warming in the oven.

12

All carving and serving should be done in the kitchen! It *looks* festive to set the roast goose on the groaning board, but in practice it is the prelude to tepid food. I have never yet known a man capable of carving with panache, or of remembering to haul out the stuffing. It seems kinder not to expect it. Under the hungry eyes of the guests, men always go to pieces, poor things, and the bird becomes a mangled wreck. Instead, I exhibit the masterpiece to general applause, transfer to a side table and dissect it myself, while the guests fill in time by passing the rolls and butter.

Similarly, I add the vegetables like a production line, and only the completed plates go to the table. Otherwise, by the time the accompaniments are handed along the line, the mashed potato is stone cold . . . and since everyone is too polite to plunge in at once, all their food is cold, too. Furthermore, someone is always shortchanged: the gravy boat didn't get that far, or she missed the celery casserole.

Infinitely smoother, then, to prepare the plates off-stage where they can be kept hot atop the stove. Then they all come to the table in quick sequence, and everyone can begin together.

No party table should ever be *cluttered*! I detest those cut-glass dishes of olives, celery, radishes to be handed about, and *somebody* always misses out on the cranberry sauce. Whap the cranberry sauce on the dinner plate as you prepare it, and dole out everything else to bread-and-butter plates before dinner begins. Set replenishment dishes in the center, if you like, but otherwise all that should ever be on the dinner table is the covered bread tray of hot rolls and a dish of extra butter . . . but I would still rather fade away to the kitchen to bring back a second batch of HOT rolls than have them cooling on the table.

The whole effect of a *party* is wasted unless the meal is carried to a smooth conclusion. No matter what the dessert, who the guests, nor how small the dining space, coffee should ALWAYS be served in the living room, with or without liqueurs, cigars and Tiparillos—but definitely with the dirty dishes, soiled napkins and half-emptied water glasses out of sight. Snuff the candles, turn out the lights, set a screen about the deadments if your dining room is only an alcove—but sweep everyone over to the couch and hi-fi music before presenting coffee.

I believe, from sad experience, that one should never permit any guest to assist in KP, particularly at a buffet party. If someone *insists* on being helpful, allow him or her to cart things into the kitchen—but do all the jettison yourself. Otherwise you will find 36 snail shells in the garbage, and granted they can be boiled sterile for hygienic re-use, it is a nuisance to be poking about for retrieval.

Above all, I believe most firmly that a party should cost no more than you can afford. Never strain every nerve by a splash that will bankrupt the budget for weeks to come! Never try to "keep up with the Joneses." It is better to offer perfectly grilled frankfurters on hot, buttery rolls, than to present lamb chops with a pitcher of *milk* for the coffee. The guest who sneers should be struck from your invitation list—unless, of course, it is your husband's boss, when you will gently, humbly, point out that the party *would* have been better, if he'd parted with a salary raise last June . . . .

An integral part of entertaining is in the appearance of the dish, no matter how simple or inexpensive. Nearly all vegetables look enticing in white dishes, particularly beets. Shrimp are somehow cooler in a glass dish on a hot night . . . and no amount of minced parsley or paprika will rescue a dinner plate of creamed chicken flanked by mashed potato and steamed cauliflower!

Food should look appetizing. If you think it looks better with candles, light some.

The Basic Theory
of Party Giving

Parties are a state of mind. Any time two or more people are gathered together, it *can* be a party if it feels like one. It is even possible to have a party for yourself alone—to celebrate a salary raise or phone call from a promising new beau, although admittedly it loses something in solitude. Still, all that's required is a nicely set table, lighted candles, the pot of African violets as a centerpiece and perhaps a glass of wine. Oddly enough, food is the least important item for a *party*. It is the air of leisurely festivity, the attractive service of the food, the faint formality of seating your guests, rather than Come-and-get-it, that labels your invitation to dinner as a dinner *party*.

For some time I have noticed that the word "party" appears to have faded from general usage, aside from an occasional child's birthday. I am not sure whether this is a manifestation of an attempt at a classless society in which the richer you are, the more you avoid any appearance of it—or timidity about an inability to meet gourmet standards, which is even sillier. How many times do you have to be told that "gourmet" is only *food* nicely cooked and served? Baked beans or boiled codfish are "gourmet" if you do them right.

Often I think the lack of parties is due to general laziness. the bus boys wash the dishes, but at today's prices you will always save money by entertaining at home, to say nothing of the leisurely chitchat following the meal . . . without a waiter hovering over your shoulder, grimly willing you to go home.

Personally, I believe in PARTIES: one or two large groups per year, with paper plates and napkins; and sit-down dinners of four to six guests once every month or six weeks. The cocktail party is a waste of time, to my way of thinking, unless everyone is "going on" together for dinner at the country club or charity ball. You must still serve plenty of food in order to avoid tiddly guests, and just as you've got them in a festive mood, the party is over.

In the long run, it is less expensive to offer a main entrée with salads than the cost of extra fancy appetizers and liquor—and nothing is simpler, if you use your head and refuse to be intimidated by the thought of *twenty* PEOPLE. The whole thing is a matter of planning and doing as much as possible beforehand. If you have someone to help, lucky you! If, like myself, you have only a man to dress the front of the house with drinks and conversation, while all the preparation is up to you, then—by easy stages—the progress of a buffet party goes like this:

1. *Choose the date and make a list of the guests.* You may have a number who already know each other, but you should always try to have one or two couples who are strangers. You will have to take special care of them on arrival, making sure they meet the old friends and are comfortably settled, but otherwise your party will turn into an ordinary gabfest in which there is nothing new or titillating.

2. *Count the forks, spoons, glasses and coffee cups.*

3. *Adjust the guest list to your equipment, or arrange to borrow for the party.* One Christmas Eve in Hollywood I realized I had 40 people expected for Christmas buffet and only 33 forks, if I pressed the kitchen silver into use. That was also the year the "insinkerator" stopped up at 6 pm, and both sinks were full of floating garbage. The landlord's wife was so relieved that I did NOT expect the impossible, she lent me anything I needed.

4. *Invite the guests—and telephone is best if possible: you have instant decision of yes or no.* These days a telephoned invitation is not an indication of informality. It's the practical way to know if your party is on or off—because from experience, I've learned that if the first three have previous engagements, you should choose another time. Various emergencies will overtake the ones who accepted, causing last minute cancellations, and leaving you with a Gigot Wellington for two people. I have never known this to fail, although I'm totally unable to explain it.

5. *Make a trial run on the menu, consulting your personal file for ideas.* For 12 people, I plan:

4 appetizers—two special and two simple, served with drinks

1 hot entrée, which may require rice

1 cold entrée, which may be served as a hearty salad

A vegetable, which may be a hot casserole or a salad bowl

Hot buttered rolls, olives, pickles, etc., to suit the entrées

Dessert—something very light for a buffet

Coffee and liqueurs

The exact dishes depend on the expectable weather for that season, plus what will probably be available in market, but this is the basic working outline. For more people, you may add another simple appetizer, but for the other dishes, it is better to increase proportions than attempt an extra.

6. *Study your first draft CAREFULLY!*

a) How much can be done one or two days in advance? I am always sardonically amused by the insouciance with which cookbook ladies say "freeze until wanted." Maybe you have the space, but it would take a greased shoehorn to insert so much as an extra egg white into my freezer!

b) How many pots, pans and serving dishes will be needed to present this feast? Be wary, oh, be wary: if you schedule Plantain Chips, it conflicts with Anonymous Cheese Puffs or French Fried potatoes. You will need the deep fat fryer for everything, which will tie you in the kitchen.

c) Preparation time for each dish! Cooking times and temperatures, oven and refrigerator space, plus top burners—all are important, or you may wind up needing four ovens.

d) Similarly, the ingredients: have you enough of any special spice or herb? Dissect your receipes and list the ingredients you'll need. I take it for granted you will have all staples on hand but what about currants, chutney, Hoisin or Oyster sauce, fresh ginger? You may need extra eggs or a quart of heavy cream. This is where you decide, regretfully, "We'd better have Boeuf Bourguignonne instead of Beef Wellington." Nor should you feel at all humble! Your guests should be happy with anything you serve. After all, they didn't have to cook it, did they?

7. *There is a final factor in religious dietary laws.* Whether or not you observe any, your buffet must present something for everyone. You may know that all the guests are of a single religious persuasion, but take no chances if there is the least doubt.

There is never any problems with Jews. The Orthodox Jew literally cannot eat in your home unless you have the separate dishes and pots for kosher cookery. They do not say this. Instead, they gracefully excuse themselves from the main dinner, "It happens we must visit my mother that evening, but may we join you later for coffee?"

The younger generation is more relaxed, but you will notice that they often quietly by-pass ham or prebuttered rolls, while cleaning up the shrimp-salad bowl. Similarly there are Catholics who still observe meatless Fridays, while Zoroastrians and East Indians are often vegetarians. Moslems and Mormons do not use alcohol, although I am not sure this applies to its use in the preparation of a dish—I am not an expert on dietary laws.

The point is that a good hostess chooses her menu to allow for any unknown (to her) taboos of the guests, and this is perfectly easy to do. A good rule is: one with meat, one without, two vegetables and a fruit dessert. It holds true also for the appetizers with drinks: a pâté, a shellfish dunk with raw vegetables, a cheese spread and/or stuffed eggs, and you will have something for everyone.

8. *Now comes the final menu*. For your first efforts, this may take time. There must be no duplication or repetition of main ingredients, including the appetizers. To illustrate, here is a sample menu for twenty:

Janice's Chopped Liver Spread
Egg Dip
Cheese Crisps
Lobster Rumaki

Those were the living room accompaniments for predinner drinks, and analyze the choices: one meat, one fish, two vegetarian—and all but the final cooking of Crisps and Rumaki will be done yesterday. They were flanked with ample supplies of small rye and pumpernickel slices for the liver . . . a large mixed basket of raw celery, zucchini slices and cauliflower florets for the egg dip. The Cheese Crisps and Lobster Rumaki wait on greased cookie sheets while the guests are arriving and will require exactly the same oven heat and time (10 minutes). You will turn on the oven; when you've introduced everyone to everyone, you will whip out to stick the sheets into the heat, *set the timer*, and return at the right moment to serve forth, calmly, two delicious hot appetizers.

For a large party—which twenty people is—I split the

appetizers into several serving stations, positioned about the room. In this way, the guests can make conversation groups and still be in reach of a titbit. The hot goodies are carried from group to group, so everyone gets one. In addition, I always put nibbles in out-of-the-way spots: bowls of mixed black and green olives, saucers of salted nuts or little cocktail crackers on small tables—so there'll always be something handy.

Dinner itself was:

Arroz con Mariscos con Pollo
Cold sliced boiled tongue with a mild mustard sauce
Mixed vegetable salad, with rolls and butter
Cole slaw
Fresh fruit compote in Kirsch
Coffee and liqueurs

Analyze again, and you'll see there is no repetition of flavors or textures. The chopped liver is a spread for bread or crackers; the vegetables to accompany the egg dip are not emphasized in the salad. Although the entrée combines fish with chicken, lobster is not used, and the Cheese Crisps are a complete change of pace.

In the main dishes, the entrée is all-inclusive with rice, and the first time an alcoholic flavoring appears is in the dessert. Nearly everything can be done one or two days ahead. What is principally needed is refrigerator space for all those tightly covered bowls of appetizers and salad components. The last minute operations are reduced to baking the two hot appetizers, completing the main dish and hauling things from the fridge. It will take 10-15 minutes for the Crisps and Rumaki; it will take 40-50 minutes to get the entrée to the buffet table—most of the time it is sitting in the oven unobserved. While you are getting it out for serving and combining the salad ingredients, you will heat the rolls—and there you are: a party.

So a vital part of it is not really cookery at all, but calm planning beforehand. You will naturally wish to put your best foot forward and convince all guests you are the best cook in this hemisphere, but restrain yourself! Never give yourself a problem by more than one critical dish. Steaks, soufflés, zabaglione—these require undivided attention and are not suitable for a buffet unless you have dependable help behind the scenes. Some part of a festive atmosphere is lost when the hostess is immured in the kitchen for more than five or ten minutes at a time. The guests begin to feel guilty for causing so much apparent trouble.

9. *Type (or write) the menu on one sheet of paper, to be pinned somewhere in the kitchen.* You may be able to keep family menus in your head throughout the week, but guests are different. To this day, I write it out in detail and hang it on the fridge with a magnetic clip. Otherwise I will forget to heat the rolls or serve the salad.

10. *Type (or write out) every recipe on another few sheets of paper.* This avoids turning pages back and forth in four different cookbooks—and the concomitant spills or stains.

11. *Make an exact marketing list.* Divide the list to indicate what must be ordered the morning of the party to ensure freshness and everything else that can be gotten 2-3 days ahead.

12. *Make an exact time schedule.* "Tuesday—market; Wednesday—cook the tongue, hardboil eggs, make cheese pastry . . ." And so forth, right down to when to remove things from the fridge on the night of the party. Be sure to allow time for you to shower and dress!

The dinner hour for a sit-down party is chosen by the hostess, and guests are invited for thirty minutes to one hour in advance, based on what, or if, they drink. I have several friends who do not use alcohol, a number who prefer sherry to liquor, and thirty minutes is quite long enough to chat in the living room over fruit juice or wine. For alcoholic drinks, allow one hour plus *filling* tidbits (see 14).

Buffet service, however, is dependent on the guests.

There are more of them, wishing to get acquainted, and some will arrive later than others. Allow a full hour, and choose an entrée that can be held an extra thirty minutes (again, see 14). In your planning, do not forget that it will take 15-20 minutes just to get everything to the buffet table.

Of course, there *are* hostesses who develop a standard menu. If invited to Rosalie's, I know it will be Beef Stroganoff with noodle casserole and a molded vegetable salad. In twelve years, it has never been anything else. I am not disappointed, it is very edible—but somehow I'd like to be surprised occasionally. This leads to . . .

13. *Keep a record of what you served to whom.* High society does this down to the color of the flowers, and who sat beside whom. I can't be bothered with that. I type the menu on a binder sheet; when it's unpinned from the kitchen refrigerator clip, it's ready to file. It is also a time-saver for the future: you have a menu that worked well, it can be repeated for different guests. Just be sure you add the new date and names.

14. Comes now the disquisition on alcohol: *It is as the laws of the Medes and the Persians that NO host or hostess ever permits a guest to get drunk.* Happy, *sí* . . . drunk, *NEVER!*

For some time I enjoyed the dubious distinction of being almost the only hostess in Hollywood at whose parties nobody got drunk. The police force loved me dearly, because they never had to keep an eye on Mrs. Lee's parties: everybody was always in shape to drive.

This stems from my father's words of wisdom when I set up my first, small, solo apartment. He said: "Pick the liquor you like, whether Scotch, whiskey or gin. Drink it on the rocks with a water chaser, or mixed with club soda. *Never* use sweetened mixers such as ginger ale, and *never* drink cocktails." Since he was my father, I believed him. It was some years before it dawned on me that *he* never drank anything but rye with ginger ale and Manhattans, but by then I was used to Scotch with water. I have never in my life been drunk, and the only hangover I ever experienced was from mixing brands of champagne (which is a special hazard, I'll tell you later).

Nevertheless, daddy was right, and if you are smart you will adopt my policy of "no cocktails" at a buffet party.

There are some other tricks: use *large*, double old-fashioned glasses with plenty of ice. The guests will gulp down about half at first, then slack off, but what remains before he feels legitimately entitled to a refill will be mostly ice water. In my house you may have any variety of hard liquor, but I literally have nothing out of which to make a cocktail. There is Bitter Lemon and Tonic to go with gin or vodka; there is club soda for rye, Bourbon or Scotch, and there is always plenty of ice.

What there is NOT is ginger ale, cokes, or rum for drinking. The vermouth and bitters are in short supply, to be used only for cooking. I do not even have the proper glasses for cocktails, let alone the embellishments of onions, cherries, strips of lemon peel. I am (mildly) regretful, but that's the way it is. My guests will get two good snorts before dinner—because nearly all of them have a head start, and have NOT had any food since lunch, which was five hours ago.

Don't you know everyone had a small snifter while getting dressed to come to the party? Because it IS a party, and already they are feeling festive . . .

This is why your appetizers must be filling, and you must see to it that everyone eats. They will, if there are allurements on nearby tables; they won't, if it means thrusting through a crowd around the bar table.

Do not be Johnny-on-the-spot for refill the *instant* a glass is empty. Allow five, even ten minutes to elapse, while carting about the trays of canapés or hot hors d'oeuvres. Then refill the glasses, and quietly apply yourself to finalizing dinner, so that it will be ready just as the second drink is finished. And while everyone is headed for the buffet, you swiftly collect all glasses left behind to be transferred to the kitchen for laundering. Later they will be ready for a nightcap.

That is the way to handle a buffet—and needless to say, if there are any teetotallers, you will have (surprise, surprise!) a large bottle of tomato juice in the fridge, a few 7-Ups, even some ginger ale that got pushed into a dark corner.

For a small sit-down dinner, two cocktails are permissible, if anyone *insists,* such as your husband, who fancies "His Special." Personally, I loathe cocktails; I can tolerate a Scotch old-fashioned, but otherwise NO. I find more and more people are adopting this method of drinking—asking for liquor on the rocks—but you must still keep your weather eye open. Two drinks of any kind are enough before dinner. You must be ready to serve the food exactly as the refill glasses are emptied.

Wine is served with a sit-down dinner, not with a buffet. Where would anyone put the glasses? I allow two bottles for four to six people; if there is any left over, I use it up in cooking. The old idea of white wine for fish and poultry, red wine for red meat, no longer applies—I don't know why it ever did, aside from cooking. In the kitchen, red wine may produce an unattractive color in a fish dish, and a white wine may not be robust enough to flavor a meat dish. At table, however, any wine that pleases your taste buds is acceptable. It goes only with the main course, although I have it poured while the appetizer or soup cups are being removed.

Frankly, I detest sparkling wines. I have, ever since my first encounter with a Sparkling Burgundy in Montreal 45 years ago; but occasionally one is forced to drink Champagne at a wedding reception. One glass is sufficient for me—but no matter how much or little you drink, if you go on for nightcaps elsewhere, do NOT order champagne.

Switch back to your preferred hard liquor tipple. NO cocktails!

You can drink any sort of liquor bottled in any year . . . you can drink different vintages of Burgundy, Chablis, Sauterne, or whatever, even at the same dinner party . . . but if you have so much as one glass of champagne that is a different year or *cru* from what you had before, you will find "little green men" stabbing your eyeballs with tridents tomorrow morning. This is because champagne is a "fortified" drink: it is grape wine mixed with brandy, and each year is a separate mixture. None of the years or *crus* agree with each other. No matter how expensive, do NOT follow a glass of Veuve Clicquot with one of Château d'Yquem, even of the same vintage year. I'm warning you; you'll be sorry.

On the other hand, if you start and continue on a single vintage *cru*, it is possible to become exhilirated without drunkenness, and to reproduce this pleasant effect for the next one or two days, merely by having a glass of cold water on rising in the morning. I toss this in out of a sense of responsibility to the younger generation, because the proper use of alcohol seems not very well understood these days.

Liquor and wine have two objectives: one is to relax tensions and stimulate the appetite, for which two drinks suffice; the other (at table) is to clear the taste buds for better enjoyment of good food. A Vinaigrette salad dressing does the same thing, which is why (if salad is served as a separate course) one removes the wine glasses with the dinner plates.

In the last analysis, I am not about to prepare dinner for a group of people who are too stoned to appreciate it!

When dinner is ended, when coffee has been served with a choice of liqueurs and when everyone has been sitting, feeling replete for about an hour, I suggest a stirrup cup of whatever liquor a guest began with. By then, he's had enough food to coat the stomach lining and can absorb one more without danger to himself or the populace on his way home.

These points constitute the basic theory of giving a party everyone will enjoy, including you. There is no reason to feel timid or inept about PARTIES. All they require is a little prior organization. And you're as intelligent as anybody else, for heaven's sake, aren't you?

Equipment and Service

For the sit-down dinner party, whatever is in the silver chest or china closet will do, and never be apologetic if dishes or flatware don't match. In forty years, I have never had a complete *set* of anything, but what of it? Does it destroy the appetite if the salad plates differ from the dinner, or if your neighbor's fork is not the same pattern as yours? I'm inclined to feel that a tablecloth, rather than mats, and large damask napkins are needed to create the right atmosphere for a dinner party. Candles also seem essential to me, but there should be some soft, auxiliary lighting. Any man likes to see what he's eating; woman do, too.

One does need a few special pots and pans, extra serving implements, to present a buffet for twenty people, but much of what's required can also be frequently used for family meals as well.

27

CHAFING DISHES

One, perhaps two, for fondues and rabbits, midnight suppers or fancy appetizers. If you have a table pot for Fondue Bourguignonne, you can improvise an ersatz chafing dish. I notice any number of fancy little pots advertised these days as for "fondue." Well, they are not for the cheese variety, and don't try it or you will end with a bottom sludge that is nearly as hard to remove as epoxy.

The true chafing dish is composed of a pan of warm water set over an alcohol flame and set beneath a tightfitting second pan in which you are stirring delectable goodies. It should have a cover so that you can let the goodie simmer, and it *must* have an adjustable flame! Many of the so-called fondue pots have only a small flange of metal to set over the burner. This type is no good even for Fondue Bourguignonne. It makes the remaining heat one-sided, and you must stir constantly to prevent scorching part of the food while the rest isn't getting cooked. If the pot contains oil/butter for beef or shrimp, it's even worse to have lopsided heat. That concentration can cause spontaneous combustion. I KNOW!

Strictly speaking, a chafing dish is a double boiler to be used at the table but it is flattish so the heat will spread quickly. A kitchen double boiler is not the same, although it can be used if you start it on the stove, and bring it to the table burner when the water has reached simmering.

I consider a proper chafing dish valuable for any home. It may be a nuisance to store, but you can set it naked and unashamed on any side table, if necessary. Mine lived on top of the piano for some years. Do not economize on the chafing dish. It needn't be a fancy design or sterling silver; it should be 2½- to 3-quart in size, with a slotted flange to cover the alcohol flame—that is, one with holes all around the top edge. It will cost about $35, but it is an investment you will use for years, not merely for parties, but for family.

ELECTRIC FRYING PAN

At least one, perhaps two . . . 12 to 14 inches square, immersible, with a temperature control ranging from "warm" to 400°. These often turn up as coupon dividends. Keep a sharp eye on trading stamps or boxtops.

DEEP FAT FRYER

Electric, of course, and be sure it has a lighted thermostat that tells you when the oil is at frying temperature. The others are cheaper, but it's a terrible nuisance to keep peering until the oil is seething. The good ones cost from $30 to $35, but are very useful for stews and slow simmerings as well as the deep frying.

All of the above can be set on the buffet table, turning to simmer temperature. You can also buy an electric hot plate with a thermostat as low as 150, on which to keep warm whatever has been cooked in the kitchen.

The Sterno stove you take for picnics or camping is not to be ignored, either. You can use it beneath a double boiler containing Bagna Cauda or other appetizer sauces—just keep an eye on the water level to be sure it isn't boiling away while your back is turned.

The small hibachis are fun to look at, but not practical for large parties. I don't say you'll asphyxiate your guests, but there's enough air pollution already without adding charcoal fumes in a closed room. Hibachis are for the patio, or for a few guests gathered about the cocktail table when you substitute *half* a can of Sterno for the charcoal. It is still wise to precook partially the tidbits on your delicate, little bamboo skewers, and allow guests merely to finish the job. Frankly, I consider living-room hibachis a catch-penny, as well as electrified woks. It is not possible to achieve the quick up-and-down variation of heat with electricity, and quickness is the whole basis of Chinese cookery. From long practice, the Chinese can do it over an open flame by moving the wok aside for a few seconds at crucial moments; but for Westerners, it is better to have gas.

STOCK POT, DUTCH OVEN

These really are a nuisance to store in a modest-sized kitchen, but you must have at least one covered, big pot that is large enough for stews, steamed mussels, boiled lobsters or homemade soup. For Bollito Misto, you will need two; one should be deep, the other can be the beloved cast-iron type with a handle reminiscent of ancestral days when these pots were hung on the hob over an open hearth fire.

That's practically all the extra-special equipment you need, and all of it can be used for more than entertaining. The chafing dish will be useful for Sunday suppers of creamed leftovers . . . you can sauté chicken parts in one frying pan while doing zucchini patties in the other . . . you can be simmering a spaghetti sauce in the deep fryer while cooking the *pasta al dente* in the stock pot.

The rest of your buffet service is a matter of invention and using whatever you happen to have. In my case, this varies enormously, due to inheriting things during my life. There is a cut glass punch bowl, treasured by my mother in 1910. It weighs ten pounds when empty, but is superb when filled with shrimps cuddling over ice cubes. Someone once gave my husband a modern, wooden thing with three scooped depressions in a row; it is meant for cuff links and such, but is also perfect for curry sambals of minced nuts or raisins. Coupons have produced fancy molds for gelatin salads or desserts, and a vaguely Oriental two-pan affair for rice and chicken sitting over hot water.

Spreads are piled on odd small plates, dunks go into cereal dishes. Dipping sauces turn up in any sort of small bowl that may have started life as a soup cup. You can put raw vegetables in silver dishes, if you like, but never use your silver plates for crackers or potato chips. The least touch of salt will pit a silver surface. For all breadstuffs, I use woven Mexican-type baskets, wooden chopping bowls and even small decorated tin trays from Woolworth's. It is nice to have a large salad bowl of teak with a silver pedestal, but the biggest kitchen mixing bowl of stainless steel will do just as well.

For cutlery and flatware, you need plenty of forks and serving spoons, and these must be either silver or stainless steel for a full buffet dinner. For the large after-dinner party, toothpicks or plastic forks are adequate. I always use sturdy paper plates and heavy paper napkins if there are more than eight people . . . and this is not to save money or the rigors of dish-washing. It doesn't save *anything*. Quality paper products are fairly expensive, but they are infinitely easier to handle on the lap than a china dinner plate. If you entertain often enough, you can invest in folding tables to set beside living room chairs, or buy extra bridge tables with folding chairs, if you've storage space between parties. I haven't.

Real coffee cups are essential, with or without saucers, although I tend to feel the pottery mugs are too informal for an indoor party . . . but you cannot use paper cups. They are too reminiscent of containers brought to desks for morning coffee break.

In the last analysis, it does not matter what sort of dishes or flatware you use for a party. The guest who sniffs inwardly at pretty paper plates and mismatched forks is not worthy of the food he is presumably—if you cooked it right—wolfing down with sighs of pleasure. To my way of thinking, the immense, catered wing-ding is far less impressive than a homemade party where the hostess did it personally, for a group of people she likes whom she thinks will like each other, and for whom she provides what she can afford.

Methods:
The Half That
Was Not Told You

This is the section reprinted from SIMPLE GOURMET COOKERY, *but even if you have that, it will be easier to turn back in a single book than to refer to another one–or so I think.*

Here are various cooking methods that appear in my recipes. If you are a long-time cook, you may not need instructions—although it won't hurt to refresh your mind. We may have different understandings of "cook custard-style." Neither shall you feel insulted by my explicit directions! If you do not need them, bully for you—but no matter what your age or how long you've been cooking, you can always learn a new wrinkle.

BASIC "SAUCE"

Any time a recipe directs you to combine a fat with flour, stir smooth, and thin with liquid, this is generically good old "white" sauce, and you should be able to make it in your sleep. For each cup of liquid, melt 2 T butter and add 2 T flour; cook/stir 2 minutes over a low flame, mashing out lumps. Then add the liquid very slowly, stirring briskly to absorb each addition before the next. When all the liquid is in the pot, stir frequently over lowest heat until smoothly thickened. This is quicker if the liquid is warm, but it's not necessary if you are careful about adding the cold liquid. If to be added to a dish that will have further cooking, you need not go beyond the first smooth thickening. For sauce *as* sauce, give it another 8 to 10 minutes of very slow cooking, stirring frequently.

If the liquid is chicken or veal stock, you may (loosely) call the sauce Velouté or Béchamel; if it's milk or cream, you have Sauce à l'Anglaise . . . but the liquid can be *anything*: wine, meat or fish stock, pot liquor, pan drippings extended with wine or water, or the juice from a can of fruit. It doesn't matter; the method is always the same, and the only trick is adding the liquid slowly enough to prevent lumping while it absorbs.

The proportions are also always the same for the medium consistency; if it's 1 T each of fat and flour per cup of liquid, you will have a thin sauce as a basis for cream soups or to be further enriched by egg yolks—and if the fat-flour is 3 or 4 T per cup of liquid, you have the start of a soufflé or croquettes.

CHINESE COOKERY

Once you've got this under your belt, it's a time-saver. Most Oriental cookery is quick-quick partly due to the climate which makes kitchen stoves unattractive, and partly due to the lack of fuel. In Oriental recipes, though, vinegar is always white vinegar, and oil is always vegetable oil; they don't grow olives. They don't have much wheat, either, so cornstarch is their thickening agent. For these recipes, you must prepare everything ahead and never mind if the kitchen smells of onion. All must be measured, peeled and chopped, dissolved or mixed, before you start. Line it up on the kitchen counter, and do NOT cook a minute more than I tell you. I mean that!

CORNSTARCH, ARROWROOT, FLOUR

These must be cooked for digestibility. Arrowroot and cornstarch should be stirred smoothly into a few spoonfuls of cold liquid before adding to the pot. These are the delicate, light thickening agents. Flour is more difficult. It can be de-lumped in a little cold water, stirring smooth until it is the consistency of thin library paste; it can be mashed with butter, and added to a cooking pot to thicken with vigorous stirring (this is *beurre manié*), or it can be added to melted butter and smoothed over low heat for the start of a sauce (this is a *roux*) . . . but it must always be thoroughly *cooked*. Low heat and stirring are essential. Flour is a hover-operation, until it has blended with its host. After that, you can hold it over low heat and stir occasionally to prevent lumping.

MERINGUES

In general meringue is used in desserts. The proportion is always ⅓ C sugar per egg white; one-half or two-thirds of the sugar is beaten in, and the remainder is folded in at the end. Theoretically, the first sugar should be powdered or superfine; the rest can be granulated. The meringues *will* be more delicate, but in practice, I can't see enough difference to matter. Some recipes include cream of tartar, which stiffens the mixture to hold its shape better. Vinegar does the same thing. If not specified in your recipe, don't worry about them.

The point is that any time it says "beat egg whites to soft peaks, slowly add sugar, beating constantly until peaks are stiff," it is a meringue. You can do it with a hand beater, but the electric mixer is easier. Be sure the egg whites are at room temperature, the bowl and beaters clean and dry! Start at fairly slow speed, adding salt and cream of tartar or vinegar when the whites are frothing. Raise the speed to medium-fast for about a minute, until you have soft peaks. Start adding the sugar by tablespoons at first, increasing as it is absorbed, and raising the speed to high at the final addition. Beat 2-3 minutes more to obtain the stiff glistening peaks. If you decide to be traditional and beat in only half the sugar, at this point you fold in the rest.

In general, meringues are baked on a greased surface for about an hour at 250. If you mean to use them for ice cream Chantilly, lightly crush in the bottoms of the meringues, so they'll dry out while they cool.

1799163

PÂTE À CHOU

This is used largely for cream puffs, or shaped oblong for eclairs; small-sized it forms hot cocktail *bouchées or profiteroles* to garnish ice cream or a *gâteau St. Honoré. Pâte à chou* is made of water, butter, flour and eggs, and no matter what you will do with it, the method is always the same. Combine butter with boiling water over medium-high heat, and cook until the butter melts. Add the flour all at once, and stir rapidly until it suddenly becomes a shiny ball and slithers away from the sides of the saucepan. Remove from heat and cool. Then add the requisite eggs, unbeaten and one at a time, beating vigorously after each addition until thoroughly incorporated into the paste. Form the desired size and shape on a greased sheet, and bake as the recipe directs. In the large dessert puffs, you often find a little underdone paste inside; scoop out and discard it.

The major hazard is overbaking until the shells are hard

nuggets. Aside from the kitchen timer, inspect your puffs as they near completion. There are always beads of moisture on the sides; if those vanish before the timer rings, ignore the timer—the puffs are done.

RISOTTO

When a recipe directs you to gild raw rice in melted fat or oil, to add liquid, cover and simmer until it's absorbed —that is a *risotto*. This is the Italian name, but nearly every country has adopted the method. The proportions are: 2 T olive oil (or butter or chicken fat), 1 C washed well-drained raw rice, and 1½ C liquid—which is generally consommé or bouillon, but can be a mixture of wine and water, fish stock, or pot liquor from the entrée. Once the liquid is added and stirred about, theoretically you cover the pan tightly, and do not peek, for exactly 18 minutes. If you measure *very* precisely and keep the heat at an absolute minimum, this will work.

The Spanish version is *arroz*, which uses more fat and liquid. It must be steamed longer, and is often set, covered, in a very slow oven to dry out.

Risotto, no matter what you call it, is tremendously useful! It is good unadorned, made with fricasee or pot-roast juices. You can make it in the sauté pan drippings after you've scooped out onions or chops, and next to curry sauce, it's the best way to stretch leftovers into a meal.

TO COOK CUSTARD-STYLE

Set the casserole or ovenproof dish of food in a pan of tepid water before placing in the oven at the specified temperature. In general this method is for recipes in which eggs are to expand and puff up while solidifying with the heat. The water level should be maintained at approximately one inch, and never allowed to do more than a quiver-boil.

TO FLAMBÉ

A great many recipes tell you to heat the brandy, or to light one tablespoon and plunge it into the chafing dish with éclat. Frankly, this is nonsense. It results in a separate operation of heating the liquor when you're frantically trying to finalize everything else . . . as well as another pipkin to be washed later. What you do is use common-sense: reduce the heat under the chafing dish, sauté pan, or whatever you are using, add the alcohol and allow it to warm while you find and strike a sturdy kitchen match. You then turn up the heat and apply match to liquid, shaking the pan vigorously to encourage the flames to dance about. All that you do NOT do is to stick your head over the pan where the flames may catch your hair.

In general, results will be better if you add a tablespoon of brandy before flaming any liqueur. Liqueurs will light, but are apt to be sluggish—perhaps because of their consistency. Nothing less than 80 proof will ignite, and 86 proof is better. Buy a bottle of cheap brandy to use as a starter; all other liquors will flame unassisted. If there is wine called for in the dish (such as Boeuf Bourguignonne), put it in first, then add the brandy, warm, and allow the flames to burn out all the alcohol.

You do realize that the reason for all this is to get rid of the alcohol and leave only the taste of the grapes or the liqueur component?

TO THICKEN WITH EGG YOLKS

Whether or not the egg yolks are mixed with cream, a bit of wine, or plain and unadorned, you must ALWAYS add a bit of the warm liquid to the yolks and stir about gently until they are warmed before addition to the main pot! Far too many recipes say "add beaten egg yolks and stir constantly until blended." DON'T! This is the way you make egg threads in Chinese or Italian chicken soup . . . and if you're not careful, you'll end with scrambled eggs even then. There is NO substitute for this operation; you must add a few tablespoons of warm (never boiling) liquid from the pot to the stirred eggs, and slowly dilute until they are ready to join the main stream. You cannot be impatient about this, or you'll be sorry.

TO WHIP CREAM

Take the cream *directly* from the fridge! If it's wanted for the garnish to a dessert, have it in a chilled bowl, with the beater waiting on the kitchen table, and whip while your husband clears the last dishes from the dinner table.

Remember: Cold cream, warmish egg whites.

TO WHIP EGG WHITES (AND YOLKS)

The egg whites must be at room temperature. Cold eggs crack more neatly than warm, so it's best to separate as soon as you remove from fridge. Then let the egg whites sit covered until you are ready to beat. A dash of salt is always helpful; you won't taste it in the end product, but it will encourage the maximum effort from your eggs.

EGGS FOR STUFFING
(This one is new, we didn't have it last time)

It may seem that anyone can hardboil an egg, but in practice it is not that easy. If you cook any given carton of twelve eggs, you will sadly discover that some will shell more easily than others . . . or will have a glutinous semicooked spot in the middle of the yolk. For a party, only a baby-bottom smoothness and pure yellow yolks are presentable. The way to achieve this is to have the eggs at room temperature. With a corsage pin, gently puncture the air space end of each egg when removed from the fridge, and let them sit for an hour. This usually prevents cracking in the pot. Bring the water to a medium boil, tenderly insert the eggs one at a time on a slot spoon, and set the timer for 14 minutes. Subsequently, keep your eye on the pot!

Adjust the heat to hold the water at a lazy, very low, simmer-boil, and literally stir the eggs gently into new positions with the slot spoon (this centers the yolks). Two or three turns is enough. After the first 4-5 minutes, you may cover the pot, being sure the heat is low enough to prevent a rapid boil. Check once or twice until the timer rings.

Transfer eggs to the sink under a flood of *cold* water, and as soon as you can handle them, crush the air space end with a sharp *thwack* on the draining board. This is enough to let them breathe, so to speak, and when they are really cooled, shell at once. Some will strip placidly, but others may need to be shelled beneath a light stream of cool water that will work under the inner membrane wishing to cling to the egg white.

It is also always wise to hardboil at least two more eggs than you plan to stuff. You will find the extra yolks are needed for the *plump* effect; the whites can be minced into a salad, or fine-chopped for a curry sambal.

Measurements

In this book, I use standard American measurements:

> T stands for tablespoon
> tsp is teaspoon
> C means our American 8 oz cup
> oz is ounce(s)

3 tsp equals 1 T—and there are 16 level measuring tablespoons of ANYTHING to 1 C. Sometimes it is easier to measure ¼ C rather than 4 T; it is also easier to halve or increase a recipe by converting to tablespoons.

2 T equals 1 oz—as you can see for yourself from a glass measuring cup. It is clearly marked 8 oz—and I just told you there are 16 T to 1 C of anything.

One final measurement: in this book "pepper" refers only to *freshly ground* black pepper. Anything else will be specified, whether coarse-ground peppercorns or white—which is the only pepper I will use ready-ground. Otherwise (in case you wonder), ¼ tsp of pepper is four healthy twists of your mill.

Appetizers and Tidbits

I tend to accompany dips with raw vegetables rather than chips or crackers, partly because the dish grows messy with broken bits, but even more because guests are usually diet-conscious. They fall upon the celery or carrot sticks with cries of joy—and (touchingly) ignore the hundreds of calories in all that sour cream and mayonnaise.

While celery and carrot are standard, variety is nice: well-washed unpeeled raw zucchini, cut in ½″ slices on the bias . . . a thawed package of asparagus spears . . . peeled seeded cucumber fingers . . . fresh or frozen cauliflower florets (best to blanch in boiling water for 1 minute, then drain and chill) . . . sturdy outer stalks of endive, or defrosted baby Brussels sprouts with cocktail picks. Cherry tomatoes and radishes are a lovely spot of color, and medium-sized raw *white* mushrooms are delicious with any sour cream dip (remove the stems for another use).

Flank the cheese spreads with assorted crackers and party-sliced breads—but a great many people still spread

41

the cheese on raw vegetables. About the only thing they eat on breadstuffs will be pâté.

Unless otherwise noted, all my appetizers are for 4-6 people; anything left over can be covered and set in the fridge for "leftover party" tomorrow. Practically everything can be doubled or tripled for a large cocktail party —but be cautious: for the cocktail party, all depends on how *many* dips and dunks you are offering! It is better to have a cleaned dish quietly removed to the kitchen than half of six dishes to be eaten up later. In other words, when it's cocktails for thirty, do not make enough of *every* dish for that many people—double the recipe will allow for sufficient titilation of their palates.

Any of the following recipes will be suitable for any sort of party, but for easy use, I've tried to group them among "simplicities" to use before lunch or a small dinner party, and distinguish between the chilled spread versus the hot goodie to be prepared by counting noses. There are also the table appetizers for a sit-down dinner . . . and the tidbits to serve during the evening of bridge.

So here we go . . .

LUNCHEON AND COCKTAILS

CHINESE SOUR CREAM #1

>   3 T sour cream
>   2 tsp Hoison sauce
>   2 tsp chili sauce

Mix smoothly together, cover and chill 1 hour—for raw vegetables. It doesn't look like much, but serves 4 adequately before lunch . . . and if everybody *loves* it, you can easily whip up another small dish to replenish the empty.

CHINESE SOUR CREAM #2

>   4 T sour cream
>   1 T Oyster sauce
>   1 tsp sugar
>   3-4 dashes of Tabasco

Instructions as above: mix well, cover and chill, for raw vegetables.

BUTTERED RADISHES

>   ¼ lb butter
>   1 T cream cheese
>   ¼ tsp each: lemon juice, grated white onion, dry mus-
>   tard
>   2 dashes Tabasco or hot pepper sauce
>   12 good-sized handsome red radishes—with a bit of
>   stem if possible

Cream butter, cheese and seasonings together smoothly at room temperature; chill for an hour. Cut the radishes in half, and spread each half decoratively with ½ tsp of the butter, making a bit of a swirl with the flat hors d'oeuvre knife. Sprinkle very lightly with ground nutmeg or minced fresh parsley. Cover and chill. Serve very cold.

CÉLERI ORDINAIRE

#1: 2-3 peeled raw carrots, fine-grated
      1-2 T Sauterne mayonnaise

Sauterne mayonnaise is 2 T wine to 1 C mayonnaise, stirred smooth.

Exact amounts for the carrot purée obviously depend on how many celery stalks you mean to stuff . . . but do NOT make the carrot mixture too sloppy; it should have enough body to hold itself in place. Cover the celery stalks loosely and chill for 1 hour.

#2: 3 oz cream cheese
      1½ oz Roquefort
      1-2 T sweet vermouth

Cream the cheeses smoothly together at room temperature. Thin judiciously with the vermouth—the mixture must not be too sloppy. Stuff the celery stalks, and chill until very cold.

Variation: Substitute Chablis for the vermouth, and add ¼ C fine-chopped Brazil nuts.

EGG DIP

      4 hardboiled eggs
      8 anchovies, minced
      3 T grated white onion
      3 T mayonnaise
      1 tsp Dijon mustard
      ½ tsp pepper

Sieve the hardboiled eggs, or use the purée mill if it has a platen with very tiny holes. Combine with everything else, mixing thoroughly. You may want a dash more pepper, but NO salt! Cover, chill and serve with celery stalks.

CURRY DIP FOR RAW VEGETABLES

      1 C mayonnaise
      1 scant T of curry powder
      1 tsp each: lemon juice, A-1 sauce, Worcestershire

½ tsp each: pepper, celery seed
2 dashes Tabasco

Mix smoothly, cover and chill.

NUT DUNK

6 oz pine nuts
4-5 T plain yoghurt or sour cream

Coarse-cut the nuts, and add yoghurt or sour cream by tablespoons until you have the right consistency for a dip. Dust the top with paprika or minced fresh parsley, cover and chill. Any sort of unsalted nuts are usable, of course, but pine nuts are less common. Serve with crackers, as well as raw vegetables.

CHUTNEY DIP

½ lb cream cheese
2 T heavy cream
1 tsp curry powder
½ C drained fine-minced chutney

Work everything together until fluffy and well blended. Cover and chill overnight. WARNING: drain the chutney very thoroughly, and do not add so much as an extra minced half-teaspoonful, or the result will be disgustingly sweet.

CRAB DUNK

1 C sour cream
¼ C mayonnaise
6½ oz can crabmeat, flaked

1 T each: lemon juice, grated white onion, drained
   capers
½ tsp salt
¼ tsp pepper

For this you need the expensive tin of crabmeat, not the
shredded variety; it doesn't come out right, believe me.
Combine the mayonnaise and sour cream with all seasonings; stir smooth, add the crabmeat. Cover and chill well.
Serve with crackers—but if there are any celery stalks,
those'll go first.

WINE CHEESE DUNK

   ½ lb Bleu cheese
   3 oz cream cheese (at room temperature)
   8 sprigs of fresh parsley
   1 tsp Worcestershire
   ½ peeled large garlic clove
   ¼ C Sauterne

Crumble the Bleu cheese ruthlessly into the blender. Add
everything else, and buzz at low speed for a minute. Then
turn to high and buzz until completely smooth. Cover and
chill for three days. Stir up before serving. If needed, add a
bit more Sauterne to thin for dipping consistency—or leave
it alone to serve as a spread.

SHRIMP DIP

   1 lb cooked cleaned shrimp
   1 small peeled white onion
   1 large peeled garlic clove
   rind of ½ fresh lemon, cut in strips

1" slice of fresh ginger
¼ C white vinegar
1 tsp salt
¼ tsp chili powder
½ C sour cream

Finely *chop* the shrimp and hold in reserve with sour cream. Put everything else in the blender, and use low speed until smoothly amalgamated. Then add the shrimp and sour cream. Mix well, cover and chill. Do not think to save time by doing the shrimp in the blender! You want identifiable bits in the final dunk.

NOTE: that slice of *fresh* ginger is essential! Powdered or grated dried root will not be the same.

CLAM/CRAB DIP (VWW)

¼ C butter at room temperature
6 oz cream cheese at room temperature
¼ C Vinaigrette
10½ oz can minced clams, drained (reserve the liquid)
6½ oz can best quality crabmeat, shredded
1 tsp Worcestershire
6 drops Tabasco

Make the Vinaigrette of 1 T white vinegar to 3 T olive oil, a ¼ tsp each salt and pepper, and a tiny dash of garlic powder.

Cream the butter and cheese smoothly together, thin with the Vinaigrette, add everything else and consider the consistency: if it seems too solid for a dip, you can add 1 T of clam liquid. Alternatively, omit that liquid and spread on trimmed toasted white bread cut in quarters; broil 3-4 minutes 5" below flame until bubbling and serve hot.

STUFFED EGGS

#1: 6 mashed egg yolks
    2 chicken livers, cooked
    1 tsp hot curry powder
    1 T mayonnaise, or enough for proper consistency

Sauté the livers in 2 T butter over medium low heat, turning frequently until nicely browned; lower heat, cover and simmer 10-15 minutes until cooked through . . . OR simmer in water to cover for about 20 minutes over low heat, and drain.

Mash cooled livers with egg yolks and curry; add mayonnaise slowly—you may not need all the tablespoon or want a bit more. It must not be too sloppy. Stuff the egg whites, decorate with a tiny parsley floret, cover and chill several hours.

#2: 6 mashed egg yolks
    2 T whipped cream cheese
    ¼ tsp anchovy paste
    1 T mayonnaise

This one should be a fairly firm paste. Combine everything smoothly. If it is really too stiff, add a bit more mayonnaise. Stuff the egg whites, and dust the tops with cinnamon. Cover and chill.

#3: 6 mashed egg yolks
    2 T Roquefort cheese
    6-7 pitted black olives, minced

Combine thoroughly, and if necessary thin with 1-2 tsp of plain milk. Stuff the egg whites, and garnish with unsalted pistachio nuts or toasted almond slivers—a scant quarter cup of nuts will do it.

#4: 6 mashed egg yolks
    ½ C ground Brazil nuts
    2 tsp white vinegar
    ⅛ tsp each: dry mustard, hot pepper sauce
    ½ tsp each: salt, Worcestershire
    2 T mayonnaise

Mix smoothly, stuff the egg whites, garnish with a bit of minced parsley. Cover and chill well.

#5: 6 mashed egg yolks
    ½ peeled ripe mashed avocado
    1 tsp each: Dijon mustard, salt, pepper, lemon juice
    ½ tsp paprika
    Mayonnaise, if needed—but it rarely is

This one must be made at the last moment due to the quick discoloration of avocado. Mash the yolks with seasonings and keep that in the fridge with the egg whites. Finally mash the avocado, combine with yolk mixture, stuff the whites and decorate with a slice of ripe olive. Cover the plate tightly with Saran and chill while you are getting dressed—but serve these among the first of your *bouchées* before they begin to darken. A ripe avocado generally provides sufficient moisture to make the right consistency. Otherwise, 1 or 2 tsp of mayonnaise—but it must not be sloppy.

NOTE: any of the above can go anywhere: before lunch or a sit-down dinner, for a cocktail party or as part of a grand buffet. I think cheese spreads, pâtés, and hot *bouchées* are too hearty for a luncheon menu, although if there are men, they generally like something to stick to the ribs.

FROMAGE HINDU

    ½ lb cottage cheese
    3 T sugar
    ¼ tsp each: ground cardamom, almond extract, lemon
        extract
    ½ C chopped blanched almonds

Whip the cheese with a hand mixer until perfectly smooth. Add everything else and mix thoroughly. Pile into a serving dish, cover and chill—overnight, if you like. Serve to spread salty crackers.

GINGER CHEESE BALL

    24 oz cream cheese at room temperature
    1 C drained preserved ginger, fine-minced
    5 oz toasted almond slivers, fine-crushed

Blend cheese and ginger bits, mixing well. Form into a ball; wrap in waxed paper and chill overnight. Just before serving, discard wrapping and roll the cheese ball in the almonds to coat completely. Serve to spread plain white Melba toast rounds.

For a *VARIATION*, substitute crushed unsalted pecans for the almond coating, and minced preserved kumquats for the ginger—but remember to seed the kumquats!

CHEDDAR CHEESE BALLS

#1: ½ lb grated natural sharp Cheddar
    3 oz soft cream cheese
    ½ C pitted black olives, coarse-cut
    3 T dry sherry

2 tsp Worcestershire
2 dashes each: onion, garlic and celery *powder* (NOT
     salt)

Blend everything together smoothly; form a ball, wrap in
foil and chill for 3 days. Unwrap and coat the ball with ½ C
fine-minced dried beef—and be sure the beef is really
fine-minced! The cocktail spreading knives won't cut
through large shreds, and the guests will make a mess out
of the ball trying to get cheese without too much beef.

#2: ½ lb natural extra-sharp Cheddar
     ½ C shelled walnuts
     3 oz soft cream cheese
     ½ tsp garlic powder
     2 tsp Worcestershire
     1 T minced chives (or 2 tsp grated onion)
     2 T chili powder
     ¼ C ground walnuts

Grind the Cheddar cheese with plain shelled walnuts.
Work this together very smoothly with everything else but
chili powder and ground nuts. Form into a ball, wrap in foil
and chill 3 days. Unwrap, roll first in the chili powder to
coat completely (use more than 2 T if necessary), then in the
¼ C fine-ground walnuts.

SIMPLE WALNUT SPREAD

     3 oz soft cream cheese
     ½ tsp Angostura bitters (or more to your taste)
     2 T fine-chopped walnuts

Work the bitters into the cheese until very smooth. Add
the nuts and distribute thoroughly throughout. Cover and
chill—overnight if you like. Serve with bland crackers.

ROQUEFORT NORMANDE

½ C crumbled Roquefort
½ C butter
2 T Calvados

At room temperature, work cheese and butter together. Add the Calvados, mix very smooth and chill. Serve with unsalted crackers.

NOTE: Calvados is Norman apple brandy—you *can* substitute American applejack, but the flavor is not the same.

EDAM GOURMET

1 good authentic Edam cheese
½ C Madeira
1½ tsp ground cumin

For this you must have a reliable cheese shop; supermarket Edam will not do. What's wanted is the imported, silver-foil-wrapped $9 Edam (and it may cost more by the time this is printed).

Unwrap only enough at the top to cut off a 1" slice. With a sharp-edged spoon and *infinite* care, hollow out the cheese to leave a rind shell. Get out as much as you can without damaging the outside.

Cut the cheese hunks fairly small, set in the blender with wine and cumin, and buzz until smooth. It takes time and plenty of scraping down. Eventually, stuff back into the Edam shell; replace the top slice and pull up its foil. Wrap in your own foil, and chill for at least 3 days—4 is better. Serve with the small party bread slices as well as assorted crackers.

NOTE: Inevitably you will end with the cheese shell, and the Edam clinging to its rind. To get full mileage out of your

investment: cook al dente enough vermicelli to fill that shell
. . . strip off its silver paper and replace with fresh sturdy
aluminum foil . . . gently scoop out whatever more cheese
you can without piercing the rind. Mix with the vermicelli,
set in the shell, and bake 20 minutes at 400.

LIQUEUR CHEESE POT

> 1 lb sharpest possible natural Cheddar, grated
> 3 oz soft cream cheese
> 1-2 T olive oil
> 2 tsp dry mustard
> 2 T caraway seeds
> 2-3 jiggers of suitable alcohol (see below)

Work the cheese together at room temperature, adding
the oil slowly until you have a thick paste—you may need
another teaspoon of oil. Add mustard and caraway seeds,
working to distribute them evenly through the mixture.
Finally add the wine or liqueur by jiggers, blending
thoroughly to a fairly soft consistency—not too sloppy, but
it will stiffen a bit in the fridge. Pack into a crock with a
cover, such as a small bean pot or cookie jar. Set in the
fridge and let it ripen for a solid week.

As for alcohol: Port wine is the standard, but Kirsch,
Madeira, sherry or Cognac are a nice change.

SHRIMP MINCE

> 1 lb raw cleaned shrimp
> ¼ lb sweet butter
> 1 tsp salt
> ⅛ tsp each: mace, cayenne
> 2 T minced fresh parsley

Fine-chop the shrimp just short of grinding—take your time, this operation is essential. Sauté in butter for 5 minutes over medium heat, stirring until the shrimp is cooked without browning. Turn into a bowl, add everything else and mix thoroughly.

You may now use this as a canapé spread on fancy toast shapes, decorating with a bit of sieved hardboiled egg, a slice of ripe olive, a whole tiny canned cocktail shrimp—what you will. Cover and chill thoroughly . . . but if you are not feeling fancy, the shrimp mince can be served as a spread, and let the guests work. This explains the very-fine mincing: the end product should contain recognizable bits of pink shrimp, but must not be too large for the congealed butter to hold them together. Otherwise, you will have blobs on the carpet.

PÂTÉ ALLEMANDE

    1 lb good liverwurst—from a top delicatessen, not
        supermarket
    ½ C butter
    1 T each: lemon juice, Bourbon whiskey
    1 grated peeled white onion
    ⅛ tsp each: pepper, thyme
    ¼ C fresh minced parsley

Skin the liverwurst, mash thoroughly with everything else to make a smooth paste. Pack into a serving dish, cover and chill overnight. Serve with rye or pumpernickel party bread slices.

CAMEMBERT PÂTÉ

    ½ lb chicken livers
    2 T butter
    2 hardboiled eggs

5 oz *ripe* Camembert
¼ tsp each: salt, pepper
3 T Cognac

This requires proper imported Camembert, ripened at room temperature until runny—use rind and all!

Sauté the chicken livers in butter for 10-15 minutes until thoroughly cooked, stirring frequently over medium low heat. Set in the blender with everything else, and purée until very smooth. If the paste seems too thick—and it sometimes is, depending on how much juice you got out of the livers or if the Camembert is not really ripe enough —you may add another tablespoon of Cognac. Cover and chill for a few hours; serve as a spread with crackers.

FOI DE VOLAILLE—This is especially good for a luncheon party

1 lb chicken livers
3 T butter
1 tsp salt
½ tsp pepper
1 T fresh lemon juice
4-6 drops Tabasco
2 hardboiled eggs

Sauté the livers in butter over medium low heat for 5 minutes, turning to brown all sides. Lower heat to a minimum, add salt and pepper, cover and simmer for 20 minutes, stirring occasionally. *Grind* the livers, reserving all cooking juices—do NOT use the blender. Add lemon juice, Tabasco and minced eggs, mashing fairly smooth. Add 2-3 T of the cooking liquid to create the consistency for a spread, cover and chill several hours or overnight.

PÂTÉ CASANOVA

1 C fresh chicken livers
1 thin-sliced white onion
½ stick of butter
1 bay leaf, crumbled
½ tsp salt
1 tsp pepper
2 T Marsala
1 T Cognac
2 T butter, melted and cooled

Sauté onion in the ½ stick of butter until tender but not browned. Add livers, bay leaf, salt and pepper. Cook/stir 10 minutes over high heat until livers are well seared. Add Marsala; lower the heat to minimum, cover and simmer 5 minutes. Force through a purée mill (NOT the blender) into a bowl set over cracked ice. Stir with a wooden paddle, adding Cognac and cooled melted butter. Work quickly, until the paste stiffens slightly! Pack into a crock, cover and chill overnight. Serve as a spread.

JANICE'S CHOPPED LIVER

½ lb beef liver
2 large peeled yellow onions, minced
3 hardboiled eggs
¼ C chicken fat
2 tsp salt
1 tsp each: pepper, paprika
3 drops Tabasco

Broil the liver for 5 minutes on each side under a medium

flame until it is completely cooked. Sauté the onions in 2 T chicken fat for 10-15 minutes over medium low flame, covered and stirring frequently until they are soft without browning. Cool liver and onions.

Force through the medium platen of a purée mill (NOT in the blender), together with the eggs. Add all the seasonings, mixing well, and moisten judiciously with 1-2 T chicken fat—not *too* sloppy, although it will stiffen slightly when chilled. Cover and store overnight in the fridge.

The foregoing are dips, dunks and spreads to be served cold with drinks in the living room before the main meal. Here are the hot titbits, and many of these are last-minute, so READ the directions!

VWW CHEESE THINGS—to make yesterday, bake today

> ½ lb butter
> 1 lb fine-grated extra sharp Cheddar
> 2 C flour
> a dash of garlic powder
> 2 T Worcestershire

Cream the butter and cheese together smoothly; work in the flour and garlic powder, and finally bind the dough with Worcestershire, as for a pie crust. Form into a roll about 1½" in diameter. Wrap in foil and chill overnight. At party time, slice the cold dough ½" thick with a sharp knife. Set on an ungreased cookie sheet and bake 8-10 minutes at 400 until lightly gilded. Serve at once.

MY CHEESE THINGS

1 pkg Snappy Cheese
½ lb butter
1¾ C flour
½ tsp dry mustard
1 dash Tabasco
1 T poppy seeds

Blend cheese and butter with seasonings until very smooth. Slowly work in the flour until completely amalgamated. Form a roll 1½" in diameter, wrap in waxed paper and chill overnight. Slice ½" thick, set on ungreased cookie sheet, and bake 6 minutes at 400. Serve hot.

PHEBE'S STORAGE SPREAD

½ lb raw bacon strips
1 large peeled yellow onion
1 C grated very sharp Cheddar

Fine-chop the bacon and onion. Use the chopping bowl, not blender or grinder; you want identifiable bits of the ingredients. It's a tiresome job; I chop 5 minutes at a time and sit down in between. Finally, combine with the cheese, mixing well, and store in a tight-capped refrigerator jar. To use, spread a small dab (not too generous or it'll melt over the edges) on Ritz-type crackers. Set on a baking sheet and broil 2-3 minutes until brown-bubbly. Serve at once.

This spread keeps almost indefinitely—except that between your husband at midnight and the kids after school, it's usually gone by the end of the week.

VWW MUSHROOM ROLLS—enough for 8-10, but doubles easily for a buffet

½ lb sliced mushrooms
¼ C butter
¼ tsp MSG
¾ tsp salt
3 T flour
1 C light cream
1 tsp lemon juice
2 tsp minced chives
Trimmed thinly cut white bread slices

Sauté mushrooms in butter for 5 minutes, stirring gently over medium low heat. Add MSG, salt and flour; blend smoothly into pan juices. Add cream (see METHODS for sauce), and stir-cook for 5-10 minutes until lightly thickened. Add lemon juice and chives. Remove from heat and cool to room temperature.

Flatten the bread slices ruthlessly with a rolling pin! Spread with mushroom mixture, roll up and fasten with a toothpick if needed. Cover loosely with waxed paper and chill several hours until you can remove toothpicks. Cut the little rolls in half, set on a greased cookie sheet and bake at 400 for 8-10 minutes until lightly toasted. Serve at once.

MOULES à CHEVAL

1 lb mussels
½ C each: dry white wine, water
1 very large peeled minced garlic clove
Bacon strips—half as many as you have mussels

Clean and debeard the mussels; steam open in water, wine and garlic for about 6-8 minutes covered over medium heat. Discard the liquor and shells. Count your mussels, and lay out the bacon to cut in half. Semi-cook the bacon over medium heat for 1-2 minutes—or just long enough to render some of the grease for discard. Drain the bacon thoroughly. Finally wrap each mussel in a bit of bacon, holding it with a toothpick.

All this can be done ahead, leaving the wrapped mussels on an ungreased baking sheet. They take about 5 minutes of baking at 400, or until the bacon is done. Serve at once.

LOBSTER RUMAKI

      2 defrosted lobster tails
      ½ lb lean bacon strips, cut in half
      1 tin of water chestnuts, drained and halved

Set the lobster tails in boiling water, off heat, for 2 minutes. Drain, cool, and slice ½" thick. Combine a bit of lobster, a slice of water chestnut, and wrap in a bacon strip. Secure with a toothpick. Set on ungreased baking sheet, and place in 450 oven for 10 minutes until bacon is cooked. Serve at once.

For lobster, you can substitute cleaned raw shrimp, also blanched in boiling water, but like Moules à Cheval, the tray can be prepared ahead for cooking after guests arrive.

ANONYMOUS CHEESE PUFFS—this is absolutely last minute

      2 egg whites
      ½ to ¾ C grated sharp Cheddar
      1 C fine dry bread crumbs

Beat the egg whites *stiff* with a dash of salt, while you are heating the deep frying oil to 375.

Fold in the cheese—enough to make a fairly stiff mixture; it must hold together. Form into small balls no bigger than a walnut. Roll gently in the bread crumbs, and deep fry for 1-2 minutes. Watch 'em! They brown like lightning. Drain thoroughly and serve at once, with a bowl of minced fresh parsley for dipping into with a toothpick.

PLANTAIN CHIPS—this can be teamed with the puffs for a second hot titbit easily done when the first are gone

>2 firm green plantains
>Deep frying oil heated to 375
>Salt, curry, paprika, ground cumin (optional)

Peel and thin-slice the plantains. Deep fry about 2 minutes at 375 until lightly browned. Drain thoroughly and sprinkle with salt—or a whisper of any other spice. Serve at once.

CHEESE CANAPÉS

>2 egg whites
>¼ tsp salt
>¾ C grated Appenzeller
>Party bread slices (rye) or thin-sliced French bread

Beat the egg whites and salt stiff. Fold in ½ C of the cheese, pile on the bread slices. Sprinkle with remaining cheese and bake on ungreased sheet 10 minutes at 400. Serve warm.

Appenzeller is a sharp Swiss cheese with very tiny holes; you need a real cheese shop to get it. You can use sharp

Cheddar, but grate it yourself; the supermarket packages are too coarse.

BROILED WATER CHESTNUTS—this is a Ymmmm, but only for 4-6 people

> 1 small can of water chestnuts, drained
> 1 C soft brown sugar (maybe more)
> Bacon slices

What you are going to DO is to roll the water chestnuts in the brown sugar, coating thickly, and wrap in half (perhaps a third) of a bacon slice; depends on how big the chestnuts. Secure with a toothpick, set on an ungreased sheet and get 'em into the broiler at once! Set the sheet low beneath the flame for 15-20 minutes, turning once until bacon is done. You *can* bake in the oven, if it happens to be already in use—allow 20-25 minutes, until the bacon is cooked—but the important thing is to *cook at once*. If they sit more than a few minutes, the brown sugar liquefies under the bacon fat and dribbles down to a sad sludge on the cookie sheet.

HUNGARIAN HAM SQUARES

> 2 T each: butter, dry bread crumbs, grated Swiss cheese
> ¾ C minced ham
> 1 tsp caraway seeds
> ½ C sour cream
> 3 well-beaten eggs

Combine everything in the order given, mixing gently but thoroughly. Pour into a greased 12″ square pan—the batter should be fairly thin. Bake 15-20 minutes at 375. Cut into 2½″ squares—no bigger—and serve warm.

CHA SUI—this is a *specialité*, particularly for the buffet or after dinner evening party—enough for 20

> 2 lb fresh pork tenderloin
> 1 tsp salt
> ¼ tsp pepper
> ¾ tsp Wu-Hiong powder
> 1 T sherry
> 3 T soy sauce

Cut the pork tenderloin in half lengthwise. Mix salt, pepper, Wu-Hiong powder, and rub thoroughly into the meat. Let it sit for 2 hours covered at room temperature. Mix sherry and soy sauce, and anoint the pork on all sides, using your hands. Transfer to a shallow broiling pan, reserving all marinade liquid, and broil *slowly* for 25-30 minutes on each side—fairly low beneath the flame and basting frequently with the marinade. Be certain the pork is thoroughly cooked, but not dried out; allow plenty of time for the broiling, and turn back and forth to prevent drying.

Remove to a platter, cover with foil or Saran, and chill in the fridge for at least 24 hours—36 is better. To serve, slice thinly on the diagonal, and accompany with dishes of traditional Chinese Duck Sauce, plum sauce and hot mustard.

NOTE: Wu-Hiong powder is fragrant rather than spicy. An Oriental grocery should have it, and be not dismayed by the size of the package. You can use it by scant teaspoonful to rub on spareribs or chicken before roasting.

DINNER

Thus far we have had the simple to fancier to chilled dips–dunks–spreads, followed by the hot *friandises*—all intended for the drinks in the living room before a meal. All recipes will serve 6-8 people; all hot goodies can be geared for a nose-count of guests, allowing 2-3 per person. Now we come to the appetizers served at table for the sit-down party dinner, of which one of the most basic is the shrimp cocktail.

SAUCES FOR SHRIMP COCKTAIL

1 lb cooked cleaned shrimp will serve 6-8 people, depending on size of the shrimp. The smaller they are, the farther they go . . . nor should you worry if the portion looks skimpy. Plump it out with extra lettuce—because the appetizer is not meant to be a filler-up.

Whiskey Sauce

> ¼ C Scotch
> 3 T honey
> 6 T soy sauce
> 1 peeled garlic clove, pressed
> 2 dashes white pepper

Stir very smoothly together, cover and chill until serving time. This is a very thin, delicately flavored sauce—but do NOT assemble sauce with shrimp until the last moment. The soy sauce will discolor the shrimp unattractively. Mix the sauce well, and pour over the shrimp just before setting on the table.

Bourbon Sauce

> ¼ C chili sauce
> 2 dashes Tabasco
> 2 tsp Worcestershire
> 1 T each: minced celery, minced parsley
> 2 tsp lemon juice

½ tsp horseradish
1½ T Bourbon

Mix well, cover and chill. Distribute over chilled cooked cleaned shrimp on a lettuce bed in individual dishes.

Sherry Sauce

½ C catsup
¼ C chili sauce
1 T each: lemon juice, chopped green pepper, minced
    scallions
1 tsp each: horseradish, minced parsley
¼ tsp celery seed
2 T very dry sherry

Mix well, cover and chill—distribute over chilled shrimp for 6.

TORRID SAUCE FOR FRIGID EGGS—for 6

6 hardboiled eggs, halved and very cold
2 T each: butter, flour, sugar, tarragon vinegar
1 pinch salt
2 T dry mustard
1 C water

Melt butter, add flour, cook briefly and make our good old Sauce (see METHODS) with the water and other ingredients. The end-product should be thick-thin, but not stiff. Keep hot over simmering water.

Halve the VERY cold peeled eggs and set face down on a lettuce leaf for each plate. Coat with the HOT sauce, and serve at once, sprinkled with minced fresh parsley.

COQUILLES TOMATES—for 6

    1 lb bay scallops (if unavailable, do not make this dish)
    ½ C Sauterne
    1 small peeled white onion, thin-sliced
    1 tsp salt
    ¼ tsp pepper
    ¼ C water
    1 bay leaf
    ½ C butter
    ¼ lb sliced fresh mushrooms
    1 T each: flour, tomato paste
    1 C strained scallop cooking liquor
    2 T heavy cream
    ¼ C fine bread crumbs

Combine all ingredients through "bay leaf" in a covered saucepan; bring to a gentle simmer over medium low heat and cook 6 minutes. Drain the scallops, reserving liquor.

Simultaneously, sauté mushrooms in 2 T butter over low heat for 5-7 minutes. Combine contents of this pan with scallops.

Make a basic Sauce (see METHODS) out of 1 T butter with flour, tomato paste, scallop liquor and cream. Cook/stir until smooth, for about 10 minutes over medium low heat, and taste for seasoning—I nearly always want more pepper. Combine with the scallop mixture, mixing well, and pour into coquille shells. Sprinkle with crumbs, cut remaining butter into bits over the tops, and bake 10 minutes at 425.

NOTE: This makes a pleasant luncheon entrée for 4—fill the coquille shells very full, and make a fancy dessert!

SHRIMP RAMEKINS—dinner appetizer for 4, or luncheon entrée for 2

> ½ lb raw cleaned shrimp
> ¼ C butter
> 4 large mushrooms, coarse-cut
> 1 C sour cream
> 1 tsp soy sauce
> ⅛ tsp Nepal pepper
> 1 tsp paprika

Sauté the shrimp in melted butter for 4-5 minutes over medium heat, stirring leisurely. Add mushrooms, and cook 10 minutes over low heat until shrimp pinken. Separately combine all other ingredients in a pan and heat very gently over lowest flame. Add shrimp pan to sour cream sauce, and simmer 10 minutes until thick and velvety, stirring often. Spoon into 4 buttered ramekins (for dinner), dust with grated Parmesan cheese, and brown 1 minute under the broiler flame.

NOTE: Ramekins are *very* Victorian or Edwardian china dishes. I don't know if they are made these days, but I like the name. What I use are individual soufflé dishes—and for luncheon, 2 large coquille shells make an adequate serving.

CAVIAR MUSHROOMS—for 8

> 24 large unpeeled fresh white mushroom caps
> 4 oz black caviar
> 2 C sour cream
> ⅛ tsp cayenne
> 1 tsp each: grated white onion, minced scallions, lemon juice
> 12 minced mushroom stems

This is a last-minute operation because the caviar will discolor the sour cream, but you want everything *cold*. Wash and thoroughly dry the mushroom caps; cover and hold in the fridge. Combine everything else but sour cream; cover and chill. Just before serving, mix sour cream with caviar combination and apportion among the mushroom caps. Sprinkle with a few drops of extra lemon juice, set three caps on a lettuce leaf for each serving and present to guests at once.

CHAMPIGNONS RUSSE—for 2

½ lb mushroom caps
1 T each: butter, grated white onion
⅛ tsp salt
1½ T Cognac
¼ C sour cream

Sauté mushrooms in butter with onion and salt for 5 minutes stirring over medium low heat. Cool to room temperature. Add Cognac, stirring to mix well. Cover and chill overnight. Finally, add sour cream and mix gently but thoroughly. Serve at once, atop a lettuce leaf.

PÂTÉ MAISON—8-12

1 lb chicken livers
1 egg
¼ C brandy
¾ C heavy cream
1 small peeled white onion, coarse-cut
¼ C each: flour, diced fresh pork or chicken fat
2 tsp salt
½ tsp each: white pepper, ground ginger, allspice, MSG

Set everything in the blender—it will take two lots to purée—and buzz until completely smooth. Pour into a greased bread pan, cover the top with double-thickness of foil, held tightly in place with kitchen string. Cook custard-style (see METHODS) in 2″ simmering water for 1½ hours at 325. Remove and cool without uncovering. Transfer to the fridge (still covered) and chill overnight.

This is to be served in slices, either on a lettuce leaf or (thinner slices) as part of an antipasto plate. What's left will keep covered in the fridge for 4-5 days.

ANTIPASTO

This is always a matter of invention, and many of its components can be used (served in separate dishes) as part of a large buffet dinner. For the sit-down dinner party, everything can be done yesterday and chilled to the last moment—when you line up the salad-sized plates in the kitchen and proceed like a fantory production line. Scallions are at your discretion, but otherwise anything goes and much of it can be leftovers: a slice of salami, a stalk of celery and a radish, a few olives, a slice of tomato with half a hardboiled egg, a small tin of tunafish (cut in wedges, it will serve 4 or 6); a tin of anchovy fillets and a tin of pimiento cut in strips will decorate six to eight plates. In addition, a box of almost any frozen vegetable cooked crisp-tender and marinated overnight in plain Vinaigrette will fill up the chinks, or you can have . . .

ARTICHAUTS à la GRECQUE—for 10-12

1 C water
¼ C olive oil
1 bay leaf
½ tsp each: thyme, salt

¼ tsp pepper
10 coriander seeds
juice of one lemon
2 pkgs thawed frozen artichoke hearts

Combine all but the artichoke hearts in a sauce pan, and simmer 2-3 minutes. Add the artichokes, cover and simmer over lowest heat for 20 minutes. Cool in the liquor; cover and chill overnight in the fridge.

NOTE: You can substitute (thawed): tiny Brussels sprouts, French-style green beans, asparagus tips, cauliflower, or broccoli florets (cut off the long stems and save for another day).

MUSHROOMS à la GRECQUE—for 8-10

3 T olive oil
3 T water
2 peeled chopped ripe tomatoes
4 crushed black peppercorns
6 coriander seeds
1 bay leaf
½ tsp each: thyme, salt
1 lb raw white mushrooms
2 lemons

Juice the lemons and pour over the mushrooms, anointing each one individually.

Combine everything else and simmer 2-3 minutes. Add the mushrooms, cover and chill overnight.

CÉLERI RÉMOULADE—for 8-10

2 large celery knobs, peeled and cut in matchsticks
1 C basic Vinaigrette
3 C Rémoulade sauce (see below)

Marinate the celeriac slivers in the Vinaigrette, covered overnight in the fridge, stirring when you think of it. On party day, drain thoroughly and discard the marinade. Replace with the following:

3 C mayonnaise
⅔ C sweet gherkins
¼ C drained capers
2 T Dijon mustard
2 T each: minced parsley, tarragon, chervil

Chop pickles and capers finely, discarding any liquid. Combine with everything else, and coat the drained celeriac well. Cover and chill to serving time.

NOTE: Like so many other things, this doubles in brass: 1-2 T as part of an antipasto plate . . . or ¼ C on a lettuce leaf served by itself as a dinner appetizer . . . or twice the recipe presented in a lettuce-lined bowl for a large buffet.

GARBANZOS TOUT-SIMPLE—for 6-8

1 large can plain Garbanzos (chickpeas)
2 small peeled white onions, thin-shaved
¼ C minced fresh parsley
½ C Vinaigrette dressing

Drain the beans thoroughly, combine with everything else and mix to coat well. Cover and chill overnight. Use a large spoonful on an antipasto plate . . . serve as salad to accompany a summer luncheon entrée . . . or double the recipe for a lettuce-lined bowl on the buffet table.

VARIATION: Substitute a tin of drained lentils for the chickpeas, but this is *only* for the antipasto plate: serve 1-2 per portion.

Now we come to the Quiches, which are many and various, and also double in brass: either small wedges for the sit-down dinner appetizer, or larger sections for a luncheon entrée.

SPINACH QUICHE—for 6-8 as appetizer

    1 pie pan (9″) lined with pastry and chilled
    2 lb fresh spinach
    2 T chopped scallions
    3 eggs
    1½ C heavy cream
    ½ tsp each: salt, pepper, nutmeg
    ¼ C grated Gruyère
    3 T butter

Wash the spinach and discard tough stems; blanch 1 minute in boiling water and drain well. Chop fine, and drain again thoroughly. Melt 2 T butter, add spinach and scallions, and cook gently over medium low heat, stirring until all liquid evaporates—about 5 minutes. Beat eggs until very light, combine with cream, seasonings, and spinach, mixing gently. Pour into the prepared pie pan, sprinkle with Gruyère and dots of remaining butter. Bake 25-30 minutes at 375, and serve hot.

LIMA QUICHE—for 8

    2 pkgs frozen lima beans
    1 peeled white onion, minced
    1 tsp salt
    ½ tsp pepper
    1 C light cream
    2 eggs

5 bacon strips, crisp-cooked and crumbled
9" pie pan lined with pastry and chilled
½ C grated Parmesan

Steam the lima beans until very tender (10-12 minutes), set in the blender with onion, seasonings and ½ C cream. Buzz to a smooth purée. Beat the eggs well, combine with lima purée, crumbled bacon bits and remaining ½ C cream. Pour into the pie shell, top thickly with Parmesan, and bake 35-40 minutes at 350.

NOTE: This is extremely solid in consistency—you can use frozen peas instead of lima beans—but it is only suitable for a small wedge as an appetizer. At least, *I* think it's too heavy in texture for an entrée.

QUICHE AUX TOMATES—6-8 for dinner appetizer, or 4 for luncheon entrée

9" pie pan lined with pastry and chilled
½ C heavy cream
2 eggs, lightly beaten
2 T each: grated Parmesan, grated Swiss cheese
½ tsp salt
¼ tsp pepper
1 C thick tomato purée (see below)

Combine the above and pour into the pastry shell.
For the purée:

1 C minced yellow onion
2 T butter
10 medium-sized ripe tomatoes *concassé*
¼ tsp each: salt, sugar, pepper
Bouquet garni of 2 parsley sprigs, 1 bay leaf, 1 tsp
    thyme

Concassé is a single French word that means "peel and seed ripe tomatoes, discarding all extra juice." A *bouquet garni* is a mixture of herbs and spices tied in a bit of cheesecloth, so it can be removed for later discard.

Sauté onion in butter until limp and gilded over low heat, stirring for about 5 minutes. Add tomatoes and seasonings. Cover and cook 20 minutes at a simmer; uncover, and reduce to a thick purée over lowest heat, stirring often for 30-35 minutes. You can do this yesterday and store covered in a refrigerator bowl; do not discard the bouquet garni until the last moment before combining with other ingredients for the pastry shell.

Finally the topping:

> 3-4 ripe tomatoes, peeled and thick-sliced
> 2 T minced fresh parsley
> 1 tsp crumbled thyme
> ½ tsp salt
> ¼ tsp pepper
> ¼ C grated Parmesan or Swiss cheese
> 2 T butter

Cover the quiche pan with the tomato slices—depending on the size of your tomatoes, you may need an extra. Sprinkle with the seasonings, ending with the cheese and the butter cut in bits. Bake 30-35 minutes at 375 and serve hot.

CELERIAC CHARPENTIER—for 4

> 1 large celery knob, peeled and cut julienne (matchsticks)
> 1 tsp each: salt, pepper
> 2 T tarragon vinegar

Mix, cover tightly and chill overnight.

2 T heavy cream
1 tsp each: dry mustard, Worcestershire, Kitchen Bou-
    quet or Bovril
1 egg yolk
1 T olive oil
½ tsp each: salt, pepper
2 T brandy
4 thick slices of peeled ripe tomato

Mix all ingredients of cream through brandy thoroughly.
Drain the celeriac well, and coat with cream/brandy dressing. To serve, set a large tomato slice on a lettuce leaf, and
apportion the celeriac on top. Sprinkle very lightly with
paprika and minced fresh parsley. Set the plates in the
fridge for 15-20 minutes, and serve.

ARABIAN EGGS—for 4 . . . this is last-minute

4 hardboiled eggs, shelled but still warm
4 T butter
½ tsp each: salt, paprika, pepper, cinnamon—mixed
    together

Melt the butter in a small skillet. With a fork, prick the
egg whites all over. Add to the butter over very low heat,
and turn the eggs over and over and *over* leisurely, until the
butter soaks into the eggs. Add more butter if needed, and
do not allow it to brown! Keep the heat at a minimum
—about 5 minutes, until eggs are lightly gilded. Set on
warmed serving dishes, cutting eggs in half to turn face
down, and sprinkle lightly with the mixed spices. Serve at
once.

MUSHROOM SAUCISSON—for 10

>20 LARGE fresh white mushroom caps
>1 lb sausage meat
>10 slices trimmed white bread
>¼ C butter, melted

Wipe the mushroom caps with a damp cloth. Mash up the sausage meat with a ruthless fork, and apportion among the mushrooms. Set on a lightly greased broiling pan and broil under *low* heat for 20-25 minutes . . . long enough to cook the sausage. Separately, toast the bread VERY lightly and slother it with the butter. Serve 2 mushrooms on each slice of buttery toast.

Occasionally one encounters total CRISIS—when there is absolutely nothing to serve to unexpected cocktail guests or the impromptu card game, because you have cleaned out the fridge ready to leave at 6 a.m. for a camping vacation. A box of saltines plus the butter you meant for breakfast will be helpful.

CRISIS CRACKERS—for 4 drop-ins

>24 saltine crackers
>¼ C melted butter

Slother the crackers with melted butter, as generously as possible; set on a baking sheet, and top 8 crackers each with one of the following:

1:   ½ tsp cinnamon mixed with ¼ tsp paprika
2:   ½ tsp grated dried lemon peel mixed with 2 dashes of
       cayenne
3:   ¼ tsp ground cumin with ½ tsp dried grated orange
       peel

Do not go overboard on the herb/spice combinations! Sprinkle VERY slightly, merely to give a whisper. Broil the crackers about 3 minutes until lightly browned, and serve hot.

NOTE that this is expandable *ad infinitum*—and you can invent your own combinations to dust on top.

Nuts are the most useful of nibbles, but at today's prices it is wise to make your own.

CHILI NUTS—do these when you're dummy hand at bridge

   4 T butter
   1 T olive oil
   1 lb blanched nuts: almonds, filberts, or Brazil nuts
   2-3 tsp chili powder

Melt butter with oil over very low heat, using a frying pan large enough to hold the nuts without overcrowding. You may need to do two batches. Add the nuts to butter/oil, stir to coat them well, and subsequently shake/stir for about 8 minutes. Keep the heat low to prevent burned butter, and watch like a hawk for the first tinge of gold! Once they start to gild, they go like wildfire and will be overdone in a few seconds.

Remove pan from heat, scoop the nuts over to paper toweling; drain well, and sprinkle with the chili powder. If you are doing two batches, the butter/oil can be re-heated—and of course you'll only use half the chili powder for each group of nuts.

CURRIED PECANS

> 2 C pecans
> 2 T olive oil
> ¼ tsp each: garlic powder, curry powder
> ½ tsp salt

Heat the oil over low heat, add garlic powder and nuts. Stir and shake for 3-4 minutes—and pecans are tricky: you can't see when they begin to be toasted because they are born dark! They toast much more quickly than other nuts. Don't overcook! Skim out to drain on paper towels, sprinkle with salt and curry. Toss to mix well, and serve warm.

CALLALESSE—for a bridge party

> 1 lb chestnuts
> 5 bay leaves
> 1 T salt
> water

With a sharp knife, gash each nut on its flat side, making slits at right angles. Set everything in a saucepan with water just to cover. Bring to a rolling boil, cover the pot, and reduce heat sharply to simmer 30 minutes. Drain, discard bay leaves, and serve warm in a napkin-lined wooden bowl. Guests must shell for themselves—and you'd better have another bowl or wastebasket to hold the gurry.

CASTAGNE—another for a bridge party or TV evening

    1 lb chestnuts, cross-gashed as above
    1 tsp anise seed
    Boiling water to cover

Put nuts and anise in a saucepan, pour over the boiling water. Cover and cook 15 minutes at a medium boil until tender. Drain well, and serve hot in a napkin-lined wooden bowl, as above.

NOTE: All the above are easily done during an evening—all can be doubled or tripled for 8-10 people. All that's needed is to have the nuts ready for sauté or boil . . . to fade away during the commercials, and set the timer to alert you when to return for the chestnuts. You will have to hover over the sautéed nuts, of course, but they take so little cooking time that you'll scarcely be delayed in getting back to the living room.

Soups

Following the *friandises* with drinks in the living room, soup is often a better choice for the introductory course to a seated luncheon or dinner party.

LUNCHEON

In general, I prefer chilled soups served in bouillon cups, particularly for luncheon: it fills you up but doesn't stay with you, so to speak. Thus your guests will not eat so heartily as to be overtaken by somnolence during the afternoon . . . most advisable if it's a bridge luncheon, or nobody will remember what's trumps.

CANTELOUPE SOUP—for 6-8

    2 large ripe canteloupes
    1 tsp cinnamon
    4 C *fresh* orange juice (NO concentrates!)
    3 T fresh lime juice

Seed the canteloupes—hopefully, they may have some natural flavor if you live in the vicinity of a farmer's market—and dice the meat into the blender. Add cinnamon and ½ C orange juice. Buzz until very smooth, combine with remaining orange and lime juices. Cover and chill well. Garnish with fresh mint leaves, if you have them.

GAZPACHO—for 6

  1 peeled ripe tomato LARGE-sized (or 2, if smallish)
  1 large, peeled, seeded cucumber
  2 peeled garlic cloves
  ½ green pepper, seeded and cut in hunks
  1 peeled red onion
  1 tsp each: paprika, basil, sugar
  ½ tsp each: salt, ground cumin
  2 T olive oil
  ½ C consommé

Set in the blender, and buzz very smooth—you may need to do two lots.

  1 peeled ripe tomato
  1 peeled seeded cucumber
  2½ C consommé

Chop this tomato and cucumber fairly fine, and combine with the blender mixture and additional consommé. Chill ICY cold, serve in shallow soup plates, garnished with slices of radish and hardboiled egg.

COLD AVOCADO SOUP—for 6-8

  4 T butter
  ¼ C flour
  2 C milk
  2 C heavy cream

3 ripe avocados, peeled and mashed
½ tsp salt
¼ tsp powdered ginger
1 additional ripe avocado, peeled and cubed

Make a sauce of butter, flour and milk (See METHODS), stirring for 5 minutes over low heat. Add the cream and continue stirring for 15 minutes until smoothly thickened. Remove from heat and cool. Set in the blender with mashed avocados, salt and ginger. Purée until velvety smooth. Cover and chill several hours. At serving time, prepare the final avocado cubes for garnish.

COLOMBIAN VICHYSOISSE—for 6-8

1 lb peeled sliced potatoes
2 sliced leeks, including some green stalk
1 large peeled yellow onion, coarse-cut
5 C chicken broth
1 C heavy cream
2 peeled ripe avocados, mashed smoothly with a fork
½ tsp salt
¼ tsp pepper

Cook potatoes, leeks and onion tender in simmering broth for about 30 minutes. Purée in the blender, add the cream and heat without boiling. Finally combine with the mashed avocados, salt and pepper, stirring gently to mix well. This can be served hot, but I like it better served icy cold with a bit of minced parsley on top.

BREADFRUIT VICHYSOISSE—for 6-8

6 thin-sliced peeled white onions
2 peeled minced garlic cloves
3 T butter
2 cans of breadfruit, drained
6 C chicken consommé
2 C light cream
½ C minced fresh chives

Sauté onions and garlic in melted butter until soft without browning, 5-8 minutes over low heat. Transfer to the blender with breadfruit and consommé (you will need to do at least two lots), and buzz until very smooth. Transfer to a bowl, stir in the cream; cover and chill very cold. Taste for seasoning; I usually want ½ tsp freshly ground pepper —you might also want a bit of salt. Finally serve with minced chives sprinkled atop.

SINGAPORE SOUP—for 6-8

4 peeled yellow onions, coarse-chopped
2 cleaned sliced leeks, with some green stalk
2 T butter
3 raw peeled diced potatoes
3 C chicken consommé
1 T curry powder
2 C heavy cream

Melt the butter and sauté onions and leeks until very soft

without browning—15-20 minutes over low heat, stirring occasionally. Add potatoes and 2 C consommé. Dilute the curry in remaining consommé, stirring smooth, and add to the pot. Bring to a boil, reduce sharply to a simmer, cover and cook 30-40 minutes until the potatoes are very mushy. Set in the blender and purée smooth. Cover and chill in the fridge. At serving time, thin with the heavy cream, and garnish the servings with plain crisp croutons.

ICED BROCCOLI—for 6-8

1 lb fresh broccoli
4 C chicken consommé
2 peeled yellow onions, minced
2 celery stalks, minced
2 scraped carrots, diced
1 tsp salt
4 dashes cayenne
2 T arrowroot in 2 T water
1 C heavy cream

Cut the buds from the broccoli and steam tender by themselves: 15 minutes covered in a steamer over semi-boiling water. Set aside. Dice the tough stalks and cook in the chicken consommé with the other vegetables, salt and cayenne—30-40 minutes of simmer, until they are all very tender. Dissolve arrowroot in water, add to the pot and stir 2-3 minutes over low heat until lightly thickened. Transfer to the blender and buzz smooth. Chill covered for at least 4 hours. To serve, stir in the cream, and garnish each plate with the reserved chilled broccoli buds. Use shallow soup plates for this one.

NOTE: This soup can be served hot, in which case you must steam the broccoli buds at the last moment while you are reheating the blender purée with the cream. Merely reheat—do NOT let it boil!

COLD LIMA BEAN SOUP—for 6

  1 pkg frozen baby lima beans
  1 peeled sliced white onion
  1 tsp chervil
  ½ tsp sugar
  1 C shredded lettuce
  4 C beef stock
  ½ C heavy cream
  ½ C dry sherry

Combine everything but cream and sherry; simmer covered for 30-40 minutes, until the beans are very soft. Purée in the blender and correct seasoning—you will probably want a bit of salt and some pepper. Cover and chill in the fridge for several hours or overnight. At serving time, add cream and sherry, stirring to mix well. Garnish the cups with a bit of coarse-grated raw peeled carrot.

Hot soups are best in Spring or Fall, when the weather can suddenly be more nippy than expected—or occasionally in winter when it is determined to conquer central heating. Serve small cups!

CREAM OF CUCUMBER—4-6

  3 C peeled chopped cucumber
  4 C consommé
  1 peeled sliced yellow onion
  4 T each: butter, flour
  1 tsp salt
  ½ tsp pepper

Parboil the cucumber for 10 minutes in 2 C boiling water, and drain thoroughly. Combine with consommé and onion; simmer 20 minutes until very soft. Purée in the blender and return to the saucepot. Mash together flour and butter (*beurre manié*, see METHODS), and add; stir over medium low heat until lightly thickened. Add the seasonings, and taste—you may want more salt or pepper. Serve with a garnish of minced chives or parsley.

CREAM OF ARTICHOKE—for 4

    1 pkg frozen artichoke hearts, thawed
    1½ C consommé
    2 C light cream
    1 ripe avocado

Simmer the artichoke hearts in consommé for about 15 minutes until tender. Purée in the blender until smooth. Add cream, reheat without boiling. Taste for seasoning, you may want salt and pepper. Garnish each serving with ripe avocado slices.

CHEESE SOUP—8-10

    1 lb whole peeled sweet onions (yellow or red)
    8 C consommé
    2 T each: butter, flour
    1 C milk
    2 C onion cooking liquor
    1 tsp each: salt, paprika
    ½ tsp pepper
    ½ C grated extra-sharp Cheddar

Boil the onions 8-10 minutes in water to cover; drain and reserve the liquor. Add onions to consommé and simmer very tender for 12-15 minutes.

Remove the onions and reserve for another dish (add to a stew, or use for Sauce Soubise).

Combine butter, flour and milk to make a white sauce (see METHODS). Stir/cook for 15 minutes over low heat, adding the measured 2 C of onion cooking liquor, seasonings and cheese. Stir and simmer until cheese is melted.

CLAM BROTH—for 6

24 Cherrystone clams
4 shallots, peeled and minced
3 C water
2 T olive oil
3 T minced fresh parsley
1 C heavy cream

Scrub the clams thoroughly, set in a deep pot with oil, shallots, parsley and water. Cover and steam 10 minutes over medium high heat until all shells open. Remove and shell the clams; you will need 12 for your service—the remainder will be luscious for fritters or a family risotto.

Strain the pot liquor through double folds of dampened cheesecloth (or a soft old dishtowel that has seen better days). This is the only fussy part: you must get rid of every grain of sand! If you have to strain twice, DO it twice. At serving time, heat the broth with the 12 garnish clams over low flame, do NOT allow a boil. Whip the cream *stiff*. Apportion the broth into six bouillon cups, adding 2 clams to each. Top with a spoonful of whipped cream, dust with a bit of paprika and serve.

CHINESE VEGETABLE SOUP—6-8

1 lb Chinese cabbage, cut in 1" hunks
2 peeled sliced yellow onions
2 scraped thin-sliced carrots
2 slices of fresh ginger root, ¼" thick
2 T vegetable oil

1½ tsp salt
¼ C dried shrimp
6 C consommé
2 oz bean thread

Heat the oil and sauté cabbage, onions, carrots, ginger and salt until wilted, stir/cooking about 5-6 minutes. Add the dried shrimp and consommé. Cover and simmer over lowest heat for 30 minutes.

Separate the bean thread by hand and break into 2″ lengths. Cover with hot water and soak 12-15 minutes; drain and add to the soup pot for just long enough to heat through before serving—about 5 minutes.

NOTE: This obviously requires an Oriental grocery, plus commonsense on the bean thread. For some reason Oriental packages are terribly brittle—look at the amount on the package before you crack it open, and separate out what you want by eye; store the rest in a baggie for next time. If you got a few threads more than 2 oz, who cares? This is a good introduction to a vaguely Oriental-type luncheon —serve in shallow soup plates.

NUTSUPPE—for 4-6

1 T butter
1 T flour
2 C consommé
¾ C ground unsalted blanched nuts
2 C heavy cream
½ tsp salt
¼ tsp paprika

Make a sauce of butter, flour and consommé (see METHODS), stirring 10-15 minutes over lowest heat to thicken smoothly. Add the nuts—which may be any sort: almonds come first to mind, of course, but I think them a bit ordinary. Why not filberts, pine nuts or Brazils? Finish over lowest heat for 5-8 minutes, adding salt, paprika and cream merely to be heated through before serving.

SOUPE PISTACHE—for 6-8

2 T butter
3 T flour
4 C chicken broth
1 bay leaf
¼ tsp curry
¾ C ground unsalted pistachio nuts
1 tsp salt
½ tsp pepper
1 C heavy cream

Melt butter, add flour, and make a sauce (see METHODS) with the chicken broth. When smoothly thickened, add everything else and stir frequently over low heat for about 20 minutes without allowing the soup to boil. Serve at once, garnished with a few slices of ripe olive.

POTAGE TOUT-SIMPLE—for 4-6

4 peeled sliced raw potatoes
2 T butter
1 peeled yellow onion, coarse-grated
1 scraped carrot, coarse-grated
4 C consommé
¼ tsp each: nutmeg, pepper
½ tsp salt
⅛ tsp ground cardamom
½ C heavy cream

Cut the raw potatoes into spoon-sized pieces and sauté

in the butter for 10-15 minutes until gilded, stirring gently over low heat to brown without burning. Transfer to a pot with all other ingredients. *Simmer* over lowest possible heat for 20 minutes, and serve in old-fashioned shallow soup plates, if you have them.

POTAGE DU PÈRE TRANQUILLE—for 4-6

    1 large head of chicory
    5 C consommé
    1 C thin cream
    1½ tsp salt
    1 tsp sugar
    ½ tsp nutmeg

Cut the chicory crossways into strips, wash VERY thoroughly, and drain. Set in a pot and cover with 3 C consommé. Bring to a boil, reduce heat sharply, cover and simmer 40 minutes until tender. Purée in the blender, return to the pot with cream, seasonings and remaining consommé. Heat without boiling! Five or ten minutes is enough. At serving time, slice 1 T of butter into the bottom of each soup cup, pour over the potage, dust with a bit of paprika.

SCOTCH BOUILLON—for 6; this is for an elegant dinner

    2 large unpeeled tart apples
    2 small peeled white onions
    4 C strong beef bouillon
    1 C thin cream
    3 T Scotch whiskey

Quarter and core the apples; coarse-slice the onions. Set in a double boiler top with the bouillon. Cook 45 minutes over *simmering* water until very very soft. Strain; add cream, and return to a saucepan. Bring just to a boil, add the whiskey, and serve at once. It should be very hot!

AVGOLEMONO—for 4

3 whole eggs
2 egg yolks
1 T each: sugar, water
3 T fresh lemon juice
½ tsp salt
¼ tsp pepper
1 C warmed consommé

Heat the consommé without boiling. Set everything else in the blender, and buzz for 1 minute. Then, as the blender runs, slowly add the warm consommé and continue to blend 1 minute. Transfer to a saucepan over medium low heat, and stir until smoothly thickened without boiling. It will take about 5 minutes. Garnish with minced fresh parsley, or ⅛ tsp grated fresh lemon rind.

SOUPE SMITANE—6-8

6 C chicken stock
1 tsp cumin seed
3 boiled potatoes, peeled and diced (not Idahoes)
1 C each: sour cream, sweet heavy cream
1 T flour
½ tsp salt
¼ tsp pepper

Combine stock and cumin in a saucepan, bring to a boil, reduce sharply to simmer 10 minutes covered. Make a smooth paste of the flour and sour cream, working out all lumps (add the cream a bit at a time). Combine this with the hot stock as though thickening with egg yolks (see METHODS). Stir gently over low heat until it begins to thicken. Add sweet cream and potatoes; cover and hold at the lowest possible simmer for 10 minutes. Serve at once, sprinkled with a bit of minced fresh parsley or chives.

KINGSTON POTATO—4 for lunch or Sunday supper with a chef's salad

    3 leeks, sliced with some green stalk
    2 yellow onions, peeled and sliced
    6 T butter
    3 large peeled sliced potatoes (not Idahoes)
    3 C chicken broth
    ½ C milk
    1½ tsp salt
    3 dashes cayenne
    ½ C underdone firm baby peas or lima beans

Melt the butter, sauté leeks and onions about 10 minutes over medium low heat, stirring until lightly gilded. Add potatoes and broth; cover and simmer 30-40 minutes until very tender. Purée in the blender, and return to the fire with milk and seasonings, peas or beans. Heat without boiling, and serve. This is a fairly thick soup, good for a cooooold day.

BLENDER BEAN—another for a very cold day sitting around the fireplace—serves 6-8 in mugs

    4 C navy beans
    5 C strong beef bouillon
    1 tsp salt

½ tsp pepper
⅓ C dry white wine
⅓ C grated Parmesan

Soak the beans overnight in water to cover and cook tender as usual, allowing 1-1½ hours of simmering over lowest heat. Purée the beans 1 C at a time in the blender with the bouillon and cooking water, plus salt and pepper. Return to a pot over low heat and add the wine. Bring to a boil, reduce heat sharply and stir/simmer for 20-30 minutes until thick. Serve sprinkled with cheese.

LOCRO—8 people for Sunday supper before the fire

3 lb potatoes, peeled and diced (not Idahoes)
1½ C minced yellow onion
¼ C butter
1 tsp achiote (annatto seed)
2 tsp salt
Bouquet Garni: 2 bay leaves, 8 peppercorns, 2 whole
    cloves tied in a bit of cheesecloth
6 C cold water
1 C milk
8 oz grated Gruyère
1 large beaten egg

Sauté onion in butter with all the seasonings over medium heat, stirring for 8-10 minutes until onion is limp without browning. Combine with water and potatoes, and simmer 30-40 minutes until very tender. Discard the bouquet garni. Slowly add milk and cheese, stirring until smoothly melted and blended. Finally thicken with the egg (see METHODS). Heat without boiling, taste for seasoning—you may want a bit more pepper—and serve.

SOUPE APRÈS—for 6-8

    1 long loaf of French bread
    1 C grated Swiss cheese
    3 T butter
    5 yellow onions, peeled and sliced
    1 head of celery, coarse-cut, including leaves
    1 tsp each: peppercorns, salt, nutmeg
    1 bay leaf
    6 C consommé, boiling hot
    1 bottle dry white wine

Butter a big casserole generously. Line the bottom with *thin* slices of French bread. Sprinkle with cheese, and repeat until the dish is ⅔ full. Sprinkle ½ tsp nutmeg over the top, cover and set aside.

Sauté onions and celery in the melted butter with all the seasonings. Cover and simmer 5-6 minutes over medium heat. Add the hot consommé, stir well; cover and simmer over lowest heat for 1 hour. Strain slowly over the bread/cheese casserole. Cover and bake 1 hour at 400. Serve in wide soup plates, handing along the wine bottle for each guest to douse over his portion.

NOTE: This is a very solid hearty soup, marvelous for a cold Fall day after an afternoon of football or sailing. Serve it in the living room, to warm everyone up at once!

Breadstuff

Strictly speaking, bread is not exactly party food, although indispensable for accompaniment to any meal. It comes into its own for breakfast, brunch and tea, when you can take time to make special muffins or invent a topping for waffles. Otherwise, your delicious homemade yeast bread is apt to be overlooked in the gustatory joys of the entrée. Nevertheless, a great many people are learning to make their own bread in preference to the cheapening quality of the commercial brands.

YEAST BREADS: FOR BRUNCH AND TO ACCOMPANY LUNCHEON AND DINNER

The first step for any yeast dough is to prove the yeast—which means to set the required amount in a measuring cup with ¼ C of tepid water and ½ tsp sugar. Stir to dissolve—which it doesn't, but you mash out the lumps as best you can and try to amalgamate with the water. Let it sit 5 minutes, and by then it should be producing lazy gas bubbles here and there over the surface. It will look like a sulphurous marsh sequence in a horror movie, but this means it is alive. If it does not create those bubbles, throw it out and buy fresh yeast.

One thing I have discovered in practically all recipes: they ALL require more rising time than stated. This may be because the heat in my apartment is either too much or too little, and I literally have no draft-free spot approved by yeast. My doughs rise atop the heating pad set on a large tole tray atop the grand piano, with my heavy corduroy housecoat tenderly wrapped about the bowl. If you have a better spot in your house, you should check the status 20-30 minutes short of the time I tell you; the dough may do better for you than for me.

The tricky part of bread-making is in the beginning. Nearly all recipes tell you to scald milk, let it cool to baby-bottle temperature, before combining with the yeast. This takes 10-15 minutes—but proving the yeast takes only 5—and somehow you have to time it so you can add the proved yeast to the lukewarm milk at exactly the right moment. If the milk is too hot, the yeast dies at once; if the yeast has got cold waiting for the milk, it is equally discouraged. I have never found any definitive answer to this, which is why my breads are uncertain: they're very good when they are good, but sometimes the yeast didn't like me enough to rise.

CUMIN BREAD

⅓ C softened butter
¼ C each: dark brown sugar, honey
1½ tsp salt
2 C scalded milk
⅓ C orange juice

Combine in a bowl, stirring to melt the butter and blend

everything. Cool to lukewarm, while proving (for 5 minutes):

2 pkgs dry yeast
¼ C lukewarm water
½ tsp sugar

Combine the two mixtures and add:

1 egg, beaten
1 T cumin seed
¼ tsp ground cumin
8 C sifted white flour

Add 6 C flour first, stirring in slowly and mixing well. Work another cup of flour in by hand, and turn the dough onto a floured board. Knead vigorously, working in the last cup of flour for 2-3 minutes until the dough is smooth and elastic. Set in a well-buttered bowl, turning the dough ball to grease all sides. Cover with a dishtowel, place in a warm spot to rise until double (1½ hours atop the heating pad on Low). Punch down, knead 5 minutes on the floured board, re-butter the bowl and repeat the rising for 30 minutes. Punch down again, and apportion into two well-greased bread pans (9x5″), filling only half full. Cover and let rise again until double (1 hour).

Preheat the oven to 425, bake the loaves 10 minutes; lower heat to 350 and bake 30 minutes, or until pans sound hollow when tapped on the bottom. Remove, turn pans on their sides and cool 5 minutes. Turn out the bread to waxed paper on the pastry board.

Combine 2 T soft butter and 2 T honey. With a pastry brush, slother the tops of the loaves thoroughly. Let cool completely before cutting.

NOTE: This bread is delicious when toasted! Serve it

buttered for tea or mid-morning Kaffeklatsch—serve it un-
toasted with plenty of butter for luncheon salad.

SWEDISH CARDAMOM BREAD

½ C milk
10 T sugar
1½ tsp salt
¼ C butter
2 pkgs dry yeast
½ C tepid water
2 eggs beaten
5 C flour
1½ tsp ground cardamom
½ C raisins
1 egg white
2 T sugar

Prove the yeast in the tepid water with 1 T of the sugar.
Scald milk with remaining sugar, salt and butter; cool to
lukewarm and combine with the yeast. Add beaten eggs,
cardamom, raisins and 3 C of flour. Beat smooth; work in
the remaining flour by hand. Turn onto a floured board and
knead for 10 minutes. Set in a greased bowl, turning to
grease all sides of the dough ball. Cover and let rise double
(2 hours). Punch down, turn onto floured board and divide
in three parts; divide each part again into three, and hand-
roll each piece into equal strands about 1" in diameter. Braid
three strands together, pinching the ends on each other
and tucking under to stay in place. Set each braid on a
good-sized greased sheet, not too close together; cover and
let rise double (1-1½ hours).

Lightly beat the egg white with 2 T sugar, paint the tops
of the braids, and bake 35 minutes at 350.

NOTE: Make the braids fairly small, or they will slop

about untidily during the last rising. This bread has a compact texture, and is extremely good toasted.

GOLDEN CRUST

5½–6 C white flour
2 T sugar
1½ tsp salt
1 pkg dry yeast
1¼ C warm water
2 T butter
1 C sour cream
1 egg white, beaten frothy with 2 T water

Prove the yeast in ¼ C tepid water with 1 T sugar. Melt butter in the remaining cup of warm water, and combine with sour cream. Stir together 2 C flour, 1 T sugar, salt, and add to yeast and butter mixtures. Blend well, and work in 3½–4 C more flour. Knead on a floured board for 5 minutes, set in greased bowl, cover and let rise for 1½ hours. Punch down and divide in half. Roll each half to 12x5, using a floured rolling pin; then roll up à la jelly roll—the long way, if I make myself clear? Transfer to a greased baking sheet, sitting on their sealed edges. Cover and let rise 1 hour. Brush with the egg white in water. With a sharp knife, slash diagonally across the tops—3 or 4 slashes, like French bread. Bake 40-45 minutes at 375.

HERB BREAD #2 (#1 was in *Simple Gourmet Cookery*)

7½–8 C white flour
⅓ C dark brown sugar
3 tsp salt
1 tsp each: basil, caraway seed, white sugar

½ tsp thyme
¼ C tepid water
2 pkgs dry yeast
2½ C warm milk
½ C butter

Prove the yeast in tepid water with the white sugar. Melt butter in the warmed milk. Combine 3 C flour with brown sugar, salt and herbs. Put everything together and blend thoroughly, beating for 3 minutes. Add 4½–5 C flour, working in with your hands and turn onto a floured board. Knead 5 minutes. Set in a greased bowl, cover and let rise 1½ hours. Punch down and divide between two greased 9x5 bread pans. Cover, let rise double, and bake 35-40 minutes at 375. Remove from pans at once.

CHOREG—this makes a vast amount!

1 yeast cake
¼ C tepid water
2 C milk
½ C butter
6 T sugar
¾ tsp salt
7 C flour
2½ tsp anise seeds
1–2 boxes sesame seeds
3 beaten eggs

Prove the yeast in tepid water with 1 T of the sugar. Scald the milk, add butter, remaining sugar and salt, stirring until butter melts. Cool to lukewarm, combine with yeast, and add 2 C flour, anise seeds, and *half* the beaten eggs (the rest is for final glaze). Beat well! Work in 5 C flour, and knead 5 minutes on a floured board. Set in a greased bowl, cover and let rise 1½–2 hours. Turn onto the floured board and pat down to 1½″ thick; cut strips 4″ wide. Roll each strip down to ¾″ thick; and cut lengthwise into narrow ½″ strips. Braid three strips together, and cut in 2½″ lengths. Pinch the cut ends firmly and tuck 'em underneath; set the little braids on greased baking sheets at least 2″ apart. Brush with the reserved beaten egg, and sprinkle generously with the sesame seeds. Cover and let rise again for 40 minutes. Bake 12-15 minutes at 400 until an appetizing brown, not too dark.

NOTE: This sounds hopelessly confusing until you start doing it, but what you are going to DO is to work your dough in sections, because it's more manageable on the pastry board. Always cut the strips parallel to the longest side of the dough—first when you've patted down (use the heel of your palm and finish off with a whisk of the rolling pin) to 1½″ thick, and second when you've rolled a 4″ strip down to ¾″. It is better to roll as much as possible in a single direction back and forth; the longer the final strips, the easier to braid and cut into 2½″ lengths.

And as with Swedish Cardamom Bread, the smaller the little braids before the final rising, the better they will look when baked. These are good for the mid-morning coffee break, or served fresh from the oven at a luncheon or dinner party.

CASSEROLE BREAD

3 C flour
2 T sugar
2 tsp dill seed
½ tsp each: celery seed, basil
¼ tsp garlic powder
1 tsp salt
1 pkg dry yeast
¼ tsp baking soda
1 C creamed cottage cheese

½ C tepid water
1 T butter
1 egg

Prove the yeast with 1 tsp of the sugar, and half the tepid water. Heat the cottage cheese with remaining water and butter until melted together over low heat. Combine remaining sugar, 1 C flour, all herbs, salt and soda. When the cheese mixture is properly cooled to lukewarm, put everything together, plus 1 unbeaten egg, and beat for at least 3 minutes with the hand mixer. Work in remaining flour, mixing thoroughly, and set in a greased bowl. Cover and let rise double for 1 hour. Punch down, and set in a greased 2-quart casserole. Cover again, and let rise 45 minutes. Bake 35-40 minutes at 350. While warm (still in the casserole), brush with ¼ C soft butter—slother it on every *inch*—and sprinkle VERY lightly with Kosher coarse salt. A scant tablespoon will be enough, because it is much more *positive* than the fine table grinds.

PSOME

1 C milk
3 T sugar
1 T salt
¼ C melted butter
1 egg, beaten
2 dry yeast cakes
1 C lukewarm water
6 C flour
2 T light cream
¼ C sesame seeds

Scald the milk and cool to lukewarm. Prove the yeast in

the lukewarm water with a bit of the sugar. Combine remaining sugar, salt, melted butter and beaten egg; add cooled milk. Combine with yeast and add 3 C flour, beating to mix well. Work in remaining flour completely. Turn onto floured board and knead very smooth and elastic (10 minutes). Set in a greased bowl, rotating to grease all sides of the dough ball. Cover and let rise 2 hours until double. Turn onto floured board and knead 5 minutes. Divide in half, and set in greased 9″ round layer cake pans. Brush with the cream, sprinkle with sesame seeds (use more if you like them; I do). Cover and let rise 2 hours. Bake 40 minutes at 350.

SPOON BUNS

3 C flour
2 T sugar
1 tsp each: salt, caraway seed
½ tsp sage
⅛ tsp nutmeg
1 pkg dry yeast
1 C milk
2 T butter
1 egg

Prove the yeast with 1 tsp of the sugar in ¼ C lukewarm water. Warm (not scald) the milk sufficiently to dissolve the butter. Combine 1 C flour, remaining sugar, salt and seasonings. Gently put everything together in a mixer bowl, adding the whole egg, and beat for at least 2 minutes —slowly, increasing to top speed. Work in 2 C flour by hand, blending thoroughly. Spoon into 12 greased muffin pans. Cover, let rise 50-60 minutes, and bake 10-12 minutes at 400.

QUICK BREADS: BREAKFAST, LUNCHEON AND SUNDAY SUPPER

Yeast breads are impressive, but quick breads are more useful for breakfast, luncheon or Sunday supper.

BASIC MUFFINS

1 C flour
¼ tsp salt
2 tsp baking powder
1 beaten egg
¼ C milk
1 T melted butter
2 T sugar

Beat the egg, add milk and sugar. Slowly add flour, salt and baking powder, and finally the melted butter. You can use an electric mixer, but do not over-beat or the muffins are apt to be full of air channels and rather heavy! I generally do this one by hand. Pour into 6 greased muffin pans about ½ to ¾ full, and bake 20 minutes at 425.

NOTE the simplicity of this recipe: it takes 30-35 minutes overall to have hot fresh muffins for breakfast . . . it doubles, even triples or quadruples easily, depending on how many pans you have. It is even possible to produce a first batch for 10-12 guests—and produce a second batch 25 minutes later—if you have the batter waiting, and can wash and dry the pans rapidly.

FURTHERMORE, you can vary your muffins to taste, according to the flour you feel like using: merely halve the cup of white flour, and use ½ C of rye, graham, white or yellow corn meal. For blueberry, currant or raisin muffins, dredge ½ C fruit lightly with 2 T flour, and fold in by hand just before pouring into muffin pans.

COUSIN IDA'S GEMS

    1 egg
    2 C whole wheat flour
    2 C milk

In the electric mixer bowl, beat the egg very light. Add milk and flour alternately, beating VERY thoroughly. Pour into *heated* greased popover pans, and bake 15 minutes at 450. Use the wire cake tester, and if they aren't quite done, lower the heat to 350 for another 10 minutes.

POPOVERS—this is in *Simple Gourmet Cookery*, but it is SO useful, I thought you should have it.

    2 eggs, well-beaten
    1 C flour
    1 C milk
    ½ tsp salt

Beat the eggs and salt together thoroughly. Add flour and milk alternately, and beat like mad for 1 minute in the electric mixer. Pour into 8 greased *cold* popover pans, about ¾ full—and set in a COLD oven. Turn the thermostat to 450, and bake 30 minutes *WITHOUT PEEKING!*

Obviously, you can double the recipe, if you've enough pans—but you have to begin with the *cold* oven.

STEAMED CORN BREAD

    1 C white flour
    2 C yellow corn meal
    ½ tsp salt
    1 tsp baking soda

1 beaten egg
¼ C melted butter
1 C molasses
1½ C milk

Combine dry ingredients, mixing well. Beat the egg thoroughly, add dry stuff alternately with the milk, ending with butter and molasses. Stir well and pour into a greased plum pudding mold with a cover—about ⅔ of the way up the mold for three hours—as for Boston Brown Bread.

This is marvelous for a Sunday supper party on a cold winter's day—it goes nicely with an immense chef's salad to be followed by warm pumpkin pie and coffee.

BREADS FOR MORNING COFFEES
AND AFTERNOON TEAS

The tea party, as such, has mostly disappeared aside from the refreshments after a lecture at the Women's Club, but the following recipes can also be used for a morning coffee party.

HONEY BREAD—this is not overly sweet

2 C flour
¾ C dark-brown sugar
1 T baking powder
1 tsp each: salt, cinnamon
¼ tsp nutmeg
⅛ tsp ground cloves
1 C sour cream
¼ C honey
2 eggs, well beaten

Combine all the dry ingredients, stirring to mix well. Add sour cream, honey and eggs; beat thoroughly. Bake in a greased loaf pan, 60-70 minutes at 325.

ANISE TEA BREAD

2¼ C flour
2 tsp baking powder
½ tsp salt
½ C butter
1 C sugar
1 tsp anise seed
½ tsp almond extract
5 whole eggs
¾ C chopped toasted almonds

Twice-sift flour, baking powder and salt. Cream butter and sugar until very light and fluffy. Add anise seed and almond extract, then the 5 whole eggs one at a time, beating well after each one. Finally add the flour mixture slowly, mixing to incorporate completely. Fold in the toasted almonds by hand and distribute through the batter. Pour into a greased and floured loaf pan, and bake 1¼ hours at 350.

PAIN D'ÉPICE

1 C sugar
¼ tsp salt
4 C flour
2½ tsp baking soda
2 tsp cinnamon
1½ C boiling water
¾ C honey
2 tsp anise extract
3 T dark Jamaican rum

Sift all the dry ingredients together (sugar through cinnamon). Pour the boiling water over the honey, and mix to dissolve completely. Add anise extract and rum, and pour the honey mixture over the dry stuff. Mix very thoroughly. Bake in a greased 8″ square pan for 10 minutes at 450; reduce heat to 350 and bake 50 minutes. Turn out of the pan, cool completely, and wrap in waxed paper. Set aside to cure at room temperature for at least 24 hours—but 36 is better.

LEMON BREAD

6 T butter
1 C sugar
2 eggs
½ C milk
Grated rind of 1 lemon
1½ C flour
1 tsp baking powder
¼ tsp salt
1½ C finely chopped unsalted nuts
Juice of 2 lemons
⅔ C sugar

Cream butter and sugar until fluffy; add whole eggs one at a time, beating well after each. Slowly beat in all other ingredients except final lemon juice and sugar. The nuts can be anything: I prefer blanched hazelnuts, because you don't hit them too often—but walnuts, pecans, almonds, pignolias, Brazil, what you will. Chop 'em *fine*. Bake in a greased loaf pan 60 minutes at 350 until done.

Combine the fresh lemon juice and sugar, and IMMEDIATELY on removing the pan from the oven, pour the lemon juice over the bread. Douse every inch of the top! Allow the bread to cool completely before removing from the pan.

STRAWBERRY TEA BREAD

3 C flour
1 tsp each: baking soda, salt
3 tsp cinnamon
2 C sugar
4 eggs
1¼ C chopped pecans
1¼ C melted butter
2 pkgs frozen strawberries, thawed but not drained

Mix all dry ingredients together. Chop the strawberries into coarse-small pieces. Beat the eggs well. Combine everything, stirring to mix thoroughly. Pour into 2 greased bread pans, and bake 1 hour at 350. Cool in the pans for 10 minutes before turning out.

Serve at room temperature with whipped cream cheese or honey butter!

CAMEMBERT SHORTBREAD—this goes with a salad luncheon, or with soup instead of crackers—or unadorned for cocktail time.

¼ C soft butter
3 oz RIPE Camembert cheese
3 eggs
2 C flour
1 tsp salt
¼ tsp chili powder

For this, you *must* have fully ripened imported Camembert! Leave it at room temperature until it begins to run, and use all of it, including the whitish rind. It takes 3 days to get it to the right stage, and cover it loosely on the dish—so the air can reach it, but your cat cannot, or you will find him chomping blissfully . . .

Cream butter with Camembert, add whole eggs one at a time, beating vigorously after each addition. Add flour, salt and chili powder, mixing to a soft dough. Pat into a greased 8" square pan, smoothing the top as well as you can. Mark into sections about 2" square, using a sharp knife. Bake 25 minutes at 400, until lightly browned, and serve warm.

Fish–
With or Without Shell

For some reason, finny-fish is not really dinner party food, aside from an appetizer like Fruits de Mer. This is largely because anything that will be out of the ordinary for an entrée will take all afternoon to prepare, but anything else is too simple to need recipes. This is not to disparage fish—merely that it is best cooked rather plainly and served with melted butter, a bit of lemon juice, perhaps a sprinkle of toasted sesame seeds or almond slivers, and this ANY-ONE can do.

I use fish for luncheon parties rather than dinner. Nothing is nicer than fresh poached salmon with homemade mayonnaise—but *any* book will tell you how, as well as what to do with shad roe or soft-shell crabs. What I am trying to do is to give you simple recipes you don't find everywhere.

LUNCHEON

POMPANO CHARPENTIER—for 4, but easily increased for 6-8.

Pompano fillets for 4
2 oranges
1 grapefruit
¼ C brandy
2 minced peeled shallots
¼ C fine dry bread crumbs
½ tsp salt
¼ tsp pepper

First section the oranges and grapefruit very neatly, which takes time, a small sharp knife, and a bowl to catch all the juice. You must remove every bit of white membrane and keep the sections whole. Do this early in the day, cover and hold at room temperature.

Broil the pompano fillets 10 minutes on each side and remove to a warmed platter. Sprinkle them lightly with salt, pepper, bread crumbs and finely minced shallot. Arrange the sectioned fruit tastefully over the top. Heat the brandy thoroughly, apply a match, and pour it flaming over the platter—tip and tilt, spooning juices over the fillets until flames die. Serve.

PARMESAN SOLE

Sole fillets for 4
½ C soft butter
1 C grated Parmesan

Spread half the soft butter on a shallow baking pan to coat the bottom. Sprinkle with half the cheese. Arrange the sole fillets on top, not overlapped. Dot generously with the remaining butter and top with the rest of the cheese. Bake uncovered 12-15 minutes at 400, basting very frequently until the cheese is golden and crusted.

FILLETS FARCIS À LA CRÈME—for 4

    8 fillets of sole, equally sized—about 4x6
    2 peeled chopped yellow onions
    ½ lb mushrooms, quartered
    2 T each: butter, fresh minced parsley
    ½ lb shrimp, cooked, cleaned, split in half
    ½ tsp each: salt, pepper

Sprinkle both sides of fillets lightly with salt and pepper. Sauté onions and mushrooms in butter over medium heat until golden but not browned. Add parsley and shrimp, mix well and cook 1 minute. Remove from heat and spread some of the filling on the fillets. Roll up and secure with a toothpick; transfer to a baking dish. Do NOT use all the filling, nor stuff the fillets to bursting point!

Make a sauce (see METHODS):

    2 T flour
    1 C light cream
    ½ C dry white wine
    2 T Cognac
    1 tsp salt
    ¼ C water
    ½ C grated Swiss cheese

Add the flour to remaining onion-shrimp filling mixture, and stir gently over moderate heat. Slowly add the cream, stirring constantly to absorb the flour smoothly. Cook/stir for 5-6 minutes, and add everything else but cheese, stirring well after each addition to prevent lumps in the sauce. Cook over low heat until the sauce is nearly boiling. Pour over the fillet rolls, top with the grated cheese, and bake uncovered for 20 minutes at 400 until golden brown.

COD IN SOUR CREAM

> 4 cod steaks cut 1" thick
> 1 large peeled chopped yellow onion
> 3 T butter
> 2 T minced fresh parsley
> ¼ tsp each: paprika, salt, pepper
> 2 T drained capers
> ½ C sour cream
> 2 T lemon juice
> grated rind of 1 lemon

Sauté onion in butter until limp. Add everything else but fish, and simmer over lowest heat for 3-4 minutes. Set the cod steaks in a shallow baking pan, pour the sauce over, and bake covered about 20 minutes at 325, until fish is tender. Dust with paprika and minced parsley at serving time.

NOTE: This sauce is good for any boneless fish steaks or fillets: sole, boned shad, mackerel or blue . . . cut the larger fillets into serving portions, of course.

Shellfish is entirely different. It is eminently worthy of the fanciest party menu, and goes happily from brunch and lunch through tea sandwiches to hors d'oeuvres, dinner and midnight supper.

CATHY'S QUICHE AUX FRUITS DE MER—luncheon for 4

> 1 unbaked chilled pastry-lined 9" pie pan
> ½ lb Swiss cheese
> 2 T butter melted and cooled
> 4 eggs
> 2 C light cream
> 2 T each: flour, dry sherry
> ½ tsp each: salt, pepper, nutmeg
> ⅛ tsp cayenne
> 1 C fresh crab lumps
> 1 C small raw cleaned shrimp

Slice the Swiss cheese wafer thin and line the bottom of the chilled pastry. Melt the butter and set aside to cool. Beat the eggs very light, add cream and all seasonings plus flour, beating smooth. Add cooled butter and sherry, beat again until smooth. Strain over the cheese, and top with the crab and shrimp. Bake 40-45 minutes at 350. Remove and cool for 20 minutes before serving!

NOTE: For the crab lumps, you can substitute tiny bay scallops, or *thin*-sliced thawed frozen lobster tails . . . and you *can* sprinkle the top of the quiche with a bit more grated Swiss cheese, but I think it is gilding the lily.

SHRIMP ON THE HALF SHELL—luncheon for 2

> 8 *LARGE* raw shrimp—they should weigh 1¼ lb in all
> 3 T sesame oil (or vegetable, but sesame is better)
> 1 peeled pressed garlic clove
> 1 tsp minced fresh ginger
> 3 T minced scallions
> 2 T each: soy sauce, Scotch whiskey
> ¼ C chicken consommé

Cut the shrimp in half, *shell and all.* Wash or pick out the black vein, but leave the shrimp in their shells. Heat oil with garlic, add the shrimp shell-side down, and sauté 5 minutes over medium low heat. Add everything else, reduce heat to absolute minimum, cover and simmer 10 minutes, bathing shrimp occasionally.

SHRIMP OBREGON—for 4

1 lb raw cleaned shrimp
2 whole peeled garlic cloves
2 wide strips of lemon peel
2 T butter
1 C heavy cream
¼ C Pernod
1 tsp salt
½ tsp pepper

Sauté shrimp, garlic and lemon peel in the butter over medium heat, stirring 5-7 minutes until shrimp are pinkened. Scoop out the shrimp temporarily; discard garlic and lemon peel. Reduce the pan juice over high heat until it is only a few tablespoons; add cream and Pernod. Reduce heat to a simmer and stir to blend well; reduce the sauce to half, stirring occasionally. Return shrimp to pan, add salt and pepper, and simmer 2-3 minutes. Serve with plain steamed rice.

SHRIMP WITH EGGPLANT—for 6

1 large peeled eggplant
1½ T salt
2 minced peeled yellow onions
2 T butter

2 bay leaves
⅛ tsp thyme
½ tsp each: salt, pepper
2 dashes Tabasco
1 lb raw cleaned shrimp (reserve the shells!)
¾ C each: thin cream, dry bread crumbs
½ C *fumet* from shrimp shells (or consommé if you're
    lazy)
¼ lb grated Parmesan
1 peeled pressed garlic clove
⅓ C sherry

Prepare the *fumet* from shrimp shells covered with cold water plus 1 T mixed pickle spices. Cover, bring to a boil, reduce heat sharply to a simmer, and cook covered over lowest heat for 30 minutes. Strain before using.

Cut the peeled eggplant into ¾" cubes, cover with cold water and the salt, weighting down in a bowl for 45 minutes. Drain and transfer to a bowl of fresh water.

Sauté onions in butter until lightly gilded, adding all herbs and seasonings. Drain the eggplant thoroughly, and add to the pan, cooking over low heat until very soft; stir frequently. Add the shrimp, and stir leisurely until pinkened (7-8 minutes). Slowly add everything else, stirring over a low flame until the mixture thickens slightly. Set in a casserole, sprinkle with more dry crumbs, dot with 1 T butter, and bake 10-15 minutes at 350 until the top browns.

SHRIMP BRANDADO—for 6-8

2 lb raw cleaned shrimp
½ stick butter
1 tsp each: salt, pepper
2 T Cognac
¼ C heavy cream

½ tsp nutmeg
1 T lemon juice
2 T minced fresh parsley

Melt butter and sauté shrimp with salt and pepper for 2-3 minutes over medium heat until pinkened. Add Cognac and flame the pan (see METHODS). Reduce heat to a minimum, and cook 2 minutes. Add everything else, and stir gently over lowest possible heat until the sauce begins to bubble and thicken. Then shake the pan leisurely over the heat, while spooning sauce over the shrimp for 4-5 minutes. Serve with hot buttered rice.

SHRIMP BASQUAISE—for 2

12 good-sized raw cleaned shrimp
2 tsp minced shallots
1 tsp each: minced chives, minced parsley
1 T butter
⅔ C heavy cream
2 T green Izarra

Sauté shallots in butter over low heat until lightly gilded. Add the shrimp and sauté 5 minutes, turning to pinken all sides, over medium low heat. Reduce heat to low, stir in the cream, chives and parsley. Bring up to the boil, stirring occasionally; add Izarra, mix gently to distribute through the sauce, and serve with plain rice.

NOTE that this recipe can be increased arithmetically for any number of people—each portion requires 6 shrimp, 1 T liqueur, ½ T butter . . . *but* go slow on the cream for the extra servings, or you end with far too much sauce. Beyond two people, I use only ¼ C cream for every additional person.

Izarra is a Basque liqueur, rarely stocked by the local

store, but easily ordered by a cooperative manager. State-operated stores may be unable to get it for you, because of mass central buying. If so, substitute green Chartreuse; the color is not quite so pretty, but the flavor is very similar.

PAPRIKA SHRIMP—for 6

1½ lb cooked cleaned *jumbo* shrimp (or lobster or prawns)
½ C of shrimp cooking liquor, strained
4 T butter
½ small grated white onion
1 tsp sweet paprika
½ tsp salt
1 T flour
¼ C sour cream

Melt butter, sauté onion and paprika 1 minute over low heat. Add shrimp (or lobster or prawns) and stir/cook 4-5 minutes to heat through. Sprinkle on the flour and salt, and stir to delump the flour until blended with pan butter. Slowly add the strained cooking liquor and stir until smoothly thickened (see METHODS). Cook about 5 minutes over low heat. Remove and stir in the sour cream, mixing thoroughly. Serve with plain boiled rice.

COLD SHRIMP CURRY—for 8-10

2½ lb cooked cleaned medium-sized shrimp
¼ C each: minced white onion, minced peeled tart apple
1 large peeled garlic clove
4 T butter
2 T flour

1 C tinned tomatoes
1 tsp each: salt, pepper
2 T curry powder
1 T lemon juice
1½-2 C mayonnaise
½ C toasted almond slivers
½ C chopped peeled seeded cucumber
2 hardboiled eggs, riced
½ C currants, soaked in 2 T dry white wine

Melt butter, sauté garlic, onion and apple until the onion is limp but not browned; discard the garlic, and sprinkle flour over the pan. Stir well to delump over low heat; cook 2 minutes. Add salt, pepper, tomatoes and curry powder, and stir gently until the sauce thickens. Remove from heat and cool to room temperature. Measure the amount you have, add an equal amount of mayonnaise and the lemon juice. Stir very smooth, add the shrimp, cover and chill for several hours. At the final moment, stir in currants and wine, distributing well. Turn into a shallow glass dish or platter. Sprinkle the almonds over the top, and use cucumber and riced egg for garnishing around the edges.

LEONIE'S LOBSTER NEWBURGH—for 4

2 C cooked sliced lobster tails
4 T butter
¼ C dry sherry
2 egg yolks
½ C heavy cream
½ tsp each: salt, paprika
¼ tsp each: nutmeg, pepper
2 dashes of cayenne

Melt butter in a double boiler top over hot but NOT boiling water. Add lobster and sherry; cook 2 minutes.

Combine egg yolks with cream, and thicken as usual (see
METHODS). Add all seasonings, and continue to stir constantly over simmering water until smoothly thickened for
about 10 minutes. Serve on hot buttered toast.

L'HOMARD À DEUX—two for dinner

    a 2 lb lobster, cooked and cleaned (or two 1-pounders)
    1 small piece fresh ginger
    2 minced scallions
    1 peeled pressed garlic clove
    1 soaked dried mushroom, minced
    2 T vegetable oil
    1 tsp sugar
    ¼ tsp ground hot red pepper
    1 T each: dry white wine, tomato paste
    ½ C chicken consommé
    1 tsp cornstarch dissolved in 2 T water
    1 tsp sesame oil

Heat vegetable oil, add ginger, scallions, garlic and mushroom. Stir/cook 1 minute over medium high heat. Add
sugar, hot pepper and lobster meat cut in pieces; stir/mix 1
minute. Add wine and consommé; reduce heat to simmer 2
minutes. Add tomato paste and blend well. Thicken with
the cornstarch in water, stirring for 2 minutes until smooth.
Sprinkle the sesame oil over the top, and serve at once on
hot buttered toast.

LOBSTER PERNOD—for 4

    4 lobsters, 1½ lb each
    4 C water
    2 C dry white wine
    ¼ C each: white vinegar, Pernod

1 scraped sliced carrot
1 peeled yellow onion, stuck with 3 whole cloves
2 T minced fresh parsley
1 tsp pepper
½ tsp thyme
1 C heavy cream
1 T each: flour, butter
2 T additional Pernod
1 C Hollandaise (optional)

Make a court bouillon of all ingredients from water through thyme (do NOT add salt), bring to a boil and add the lobsters. Reduce to a simmer, cover and cook 15-20 minutes. Remove the lobsters, cool, and split to clean—reserve the shells (if you can; they generally fall apart with the small lobs. I think it's safer to separate tail from body and get two decent-sized shells for eventual stuffing).

Reduce the court bouillon over high heat to 1½ C of liquid. Strain, and add the cream. Mash butter and flour together (*beurre manié*, see METHODS), and thicken the bouillon, adding the 2 T Pernod. Cook tenderly until smooth, for 8-10 minutes. Add the lobster meat, cut in bite-sized pieces, and heat through without boiling for 4-5 minutes.

Fill the lobster shells, top with the Hollandaise and a sprinkle of dry bread crumbs. Glaze under the broiler for 1-2 minutes until lightly browned, and serve. If you are not feeling fancy enough for the Hollandaise, you can serve the lobster without shells on hot buttered toast. Alternatively, if the shells did not survive attractively, you can put the lobster in a suitable broiling dish and spread with the Hollandaise . . . in which case, you can probably stretch the lobster into six portions for lunch.

CRABMEAT CASSEROLE—for 4

   ½ lb sliced fresh mushrooms
   ¼ lb butter
   1 T flour
   ½ C heavy cream
   2 T brandy
   2 slices crisp-cooked bacon, cooled and crumbled
   ½ lb crab lumps
   ½ lb cleaned cooked shrimp (use small size)
   ¼ C each: bread crumbs, grated Parmesan

Sauté mushrooms in melted butter over low heat, stirring 2-3 minutes; sprinkle with flour and stir to delump for 2-3 minutes. Slowly add cream and stir to a sauce (see METHODS). Cook 8-10 minutes, add the brandy and simmer 2 minutes. Place crab lumps and shrimp in a buttered casserole, pour the sauce over; dust with bread crumbs, and top with bacon bits. Sprinkle over all the Parmesan, and bake 10 minutes uncovered at 450. Finish by browning 2-3 minutes under the broiler if needed—but it may be browned enough in the baking.

HENRI'S CRAB CASSEROLE—for 4

   2 minced shallots
   4 sliced mushrooms
   2 T butter
   1 C heavy cream
   ¼ C each: sherry, brandy
   ½ tsp each: salt, pepper, paprika
   1 lb crab lumps

2 hardboiled eggs, coarse-cut
Plain croutons—⅔ to 1 C
Grated Parmesan—2-4 T

Sauté shallots and mushrooms in butter for 5 minutes over medium low heat. Add cream, sherry, brandy and seasonings; stir to mix well. Add crab lumps and eggs; mix very gently—don't break the crab lumps. Transfer to a lightly greased casserole. Top with croutons, sprinkle with cheese, and bake uncovered 10 minutes at 400 until lightly browned.

BUFFET

BUFFET SHRIMP—for 20

4 lb cooked shelled shrimp
4 cans condensed cream of mushroom soup
3 C light cream
1 T salt
⅓ C ground dill seed
2 C toasted slivered almonds

Heat condensed soup, salt, cream and dill in a large double boiler over hot water until thoroughly blended. Add the shrimp, cover and hold over simmering water until serving time. It's that simple!

Toast the almonds whenever you like—either in the oven when baking something else (shake the pan frequently, 8-10 minutes), or sauté in 3 T olive oil over medium high heat, stirring with a slot spoon. Add almonds to shrimp mixture at the last minute before transfer to the buffet table.

Half an hour before serving time, prepare 5 C of raw rice, to accompany the shrimp in another warmed dish.

NOTE that I rarely use condensed soups, but for this sort

of dish, they are a tremendous time-saver and entirely acceptable.

LOONG HA PEEN—for 8

2½ lb lobster tails
1 whole chicken breast
2 C water chestnuts, drained and sliced
1 can bamboo shoots, drained and sliced
2 minced peeled garlic cloves
1½ lb snow peas
1 lb fresh mushrooms, sliced Chinese style
½ lb shredded Chinese cabbage
3 hardboiled eggs
1 C coarse-broken walnut meats
6 T oil
4 C chicken broth
2½ T cornstarch
½ C water
1½ T salt
1 tsp sugar
2 tsp MSG

As with all Oriental recipes, you must have everything set out like a production line before you start the final cooking—which then goes like wildfire.

Cook the lobster tails, clean and slice thin. Cook the chicken breast in simmering water with a dash of salt, about 20 minutes until tender; cool and cut in small strips. Save the cooking water, if you are going to make the chicken broth out of soup packets, and extend with plain hot water to 4 C.

Sauté the nut meats in 2 T vegetable oil until deep gold—about 4 minutes stirring over medium heat. Drain well.

Chop the hardboiled eggs very fine.

Thaw frozen snow peas, and hold aside.

Prepare all the other vegetables—they can be combined in a big bowl. Chinese-sliced mushrooms are cut from the top straight down through the stem, so the inner slices look like umbrellas.

Mix cornstarch with water. Measure the seasonings into a cup. Bring the chicken broth just to a boil . . . and NOW you can put the dish together, but you do see how everything can be done in the morning and left covered at room temperature?

The final bit is heating the consommé while you are also heating 4 T oil with minced garlic in an electric fry pan (350). When sizzling, add chicken, lobster and vegetables (except snow peas). Stir/cook 2 minutes; add warm broth and seasonings. Cover and cook 4 minutes. Add snow peas; cover and cook 1 minute. Stir up the cornstarch in water, add to the pan and stir 2 minutes until lightly thickened.

Transfer to the buffet table and serve!

Poultry

This is the major standby for any party, from brunch through midnight supper. Everybody likes chicken, although an increasing number of people are becoming valiant enough to admit they *detest* white meat, which has long been considered the fancy part. Well, I loathe it, myself; for unknown guests I buy an assortment of parts, with an extra thigh to be sure I'll get one. With roast chicken, I do my best to work off the breast meat on all the other plates, and resign myself to chicken salad tomorrow. Occasionally someone does prefer white meat . . .

LUNCHEON

CHICKENBURGERS—4 to 6 for luncheon

> 2 large whole chicken breasts
> 1 C heavy cream
> 1½ tsp salt
> ¼ tsp nutmeg
> ½ C bread crumbs
> 1 T minced fresh parsley

Bone the chicken, discarding skin. Grind medium-coarse to make 2 C of raw chicken. Combine all ingredients—the mixture should be rather soft. Form into 4 or 6 portions, and coat with more bread crumbs.

Set on a lightly greased broiling pan, dot with bits of 2 T of butter, and broil 8-9 minutes on each side until crumbs are golden brown . . . use a bit more butter dots when you turn, and handle gently: chickenburgers are much softer than hamburgers.

Traditionally, this is served with *SAUCE SUPREME,* which is merely good old white sauce, gussied up with mushrooms, egg yolks and sherry:

> 1 C medium white sauce made with chicken broth instead of milk
> ⅓ C fine-cut fresh mushrooms
> 2 egg yolks, lightly beaten
> ⅓ C heavy cream
> 3 T dry sherry
> 2 tsp lemon juice
> ½ tsp each: salt, paprika
> ¼ tsp white pepper

Cover the mushrooms with water, bring just to a boil over high heat and instantly set the pan aside, covered, off heat.

Make the sauce (see METHODS) with double-strength chicken broth (use 2 consommé packets instead of one). When smoothly thickened, combine egg yolks and cream, and thicken the sauce carefully (see METHODS again). Cook smooth over lowest heat, stirring constantly. Add seasonings, drained mushrooms, sherry and lemon juice. Spoon the sauce around the base of each chickenburger on its serving plate, and garnish with a bit of minced fresh parsley.

ROULADE—this one is tricky, but impressive for a luncheon party of 4

> 6 T butter
> ½ C flour
> 2 C milk
> 5 eggs, separated
> 1 T sugar
> ½ tsp each: salt, pepper

Filling:

> 2 C diced cooked chicken
> 2 C *thick* cream sauce
> 1 C sour cream
> Juice of ½ lemon
> 4 dashes Tabasco
> 2 dashes cayenne
> ½ tsp each: salt, pepper

Now what you are going to DO is to make a white sauce out of the first ingredients, which you will bake and cool. Second, you will make another *thick* white sauce (see METHODS) to be seasoned with the last ingredients and added to the chicken. Finally, you will spread half the chicken sauce on the first cooled baked sauce, roll up like a jelly roll, and bake briefly to gild. The tricky bit is making the roll without its falling apart into dishevelment. The remaining chicken sauce goes on top at serving time.

Prepare a shallow baking pan with double folds of waxed paper hanging a bit over the edges, so you can grasp it when you remove it from the oven. Lightly butter the waxed paper.

Make a white sauce of 6 T butter, ½ C flour, 2 C milk (see METHODS). Separate the eggs, beat the yolks and combine with slightly cooled sauce (see METHODS). Add the seasonings, and beat well. Stiff-beat the egg whites, and fold them into the sauce. Pour into the prepared paper-lined pan and bake 50 minutes at 325, until delicately golden brown. Remove from the heat, allow to cool slightly, and turn out onto a clean dish towel on the pastry board. The way to do it is to lay the towel over the baking sheet, top with pastry board, and, firmly grasping board-towel-baking sheet, swiftly upside-down it. Let it cool *completely* before removing the waxed paper!

The second white sauce for the diced chicken is 6 T each of flour and butter with 2 C milk or light cream (see METHODS). When you have that smoothly thickened, add everything else, mixing well. Allow it to cool somewhat. Remove the paper from roulade, spread half the chicken mixture along its length, and roll it up by grasping the towel to flop over, until you have a jelly roll. Slide this onto another lightly greased baking sheet, and brown 15 minutes at 325.

Heat the remaining chicken mixture without boiling —and perhaps you will like to thin down with 1-2 T milk. I usually like this topping less compact than the filling. If you survived this far, pour the hot chicken over the roulade, take it to table where everyone may applaud your effort. Then slice like a jelly roll—and it will instantly disintegrate, but nichevo! Everybody SAW you could do it.

LUNCHEON AND DINNER

PICNIC DEVIL AND CHICKEN ROQUEFORT—for 4

These recipes start the same way: enough chicken parts for 4, or 2 broilers cut in half. Lightly grease with bacon drippings or olive oil, set in a pan and bake 45-50 minutes at

350 until fork tender. Turn and baste the pieces with pan juice every 10 or 15 minutes. Then . . .

#1: Spread the chicken pieces with a THICK coating of Dijon mustard.
Sprinkle generously with fine dry bread crumbs.

Set under the broiler until crumbs brown lightly—for 6-8 minutes; repeat mustard and crumbs for the reverse side. Serve hot—but this is marvelous cold in the picnic basket.

#2: 6 oz Roquefort
1½ C sour cream
1 peeled pressed garlic clove

Mash all together to a smooth paste. Spread over the cooked chicken parts, and bake covered 30 minutes at 375.

HONEY BROILERS—for 4

2 broilers, halved
¼ C each: Dijon mustard, honey
1 T lemon juice
1 tsp salt
3 T butter

Melt the butter in a foil-lined baking pan, tilting to coat the bottom. Set the chicken halves skinside down, not overlapped. Combine everything else, blending well, and paint the chicken with a pastry brush, using about half the honey mixture. Bake 30 minutes uncovered at 350, brushing with some more honey at 15 minutes. Turn the halves, paint with remainder of the honey, and bake fork tender for about 20-30 minutes, basting frequently. Apportion the pan sauce over chicken on dinner plates.

POULET À L'AIL—for 4-6

French bread, cut ¾" thick slices to line a deep casserole
4 lb roasting chicken, neatly trussed
2 T soft butter
1 T kosher salt
2 bay leaves
3 *large* whole heads of garlic

Set bread in the bottom of the casserole and place chicken on top. Smear the chicken with the soft butter, sprinkle all over with the salt, and do not use more than that tablespoon! Add the bay leaves. Separate the garlic into its cloves, dip in cold water, but DO NOT PEEL. Be sure the garlic is fresh; supermarket packages are often dry as well as too small—Puerto Rican shops carry big frisky heads of garlic. Distribute the cloves about in the casserole, tucking around and atop the chicken. Cover and bake 1½-2 hours at 350 until very tender. Remove chicken to a warmed platter and untruss it. Skin the garlic cloves, mash well and spread on the bread to serve with sliced chicken.

NOTE: Do not be appalled at the amount of garlic. When slowly cooked, particularly unpeeled, it has a surprisingly delicate flavor.

DINNER

CHICKEN BREASTS IN CHAMPAGNE—for 4

2 whole chicken breasts
6 T butter
1 T oil

1 C Champagne
1 tsp lemon juice
2 T heavy cream
½ tsp salt
¼ tsp pepper

Bone and split the chicken breasts, pull out the tough white tendon on each half, and slightly flatten the meat with the broad side of the kitchen cleaver. Sauté on both sides in butter/oil for 15 minutes uncovered over medium heat, until gently browned. Remove to a hot platter. Add Champagne and lemon juice to the pan; raise the heat and reduce by half, stirring occasionally. Lower heat sharply, add cream and seasoning, heat without boiling, and pour over the chicken.

FOIE GRAS BROILER—for 2

1 broiler, cut in half
¼ C butter, melted
3 oz foie gras
½ C heavy cream
1 C dry bread crumbs

Using half the melted butter, brush both sides of broiler sections and set skinside down on the broiler pan, 5″ below flame. Turn the chicken every 15 minutes for 1 hour, brushing with remaining butter at the halfway point, until fork tender. Remove and keep warm.

Mash cream and foie gras together very smoothly; spread on cooked chicken, sprinkle generously with crumbs and return to the broiler flame for 5-6 minutes until crumbs brown lightly.

CHICKEN TAIWAN—for 4

1 large whole chicken breast (or 2, if small)
4 T oil
1 large peeled garlic clove, minced
¾ tsp salt
2 T soy sauce
1 C peeled yellow onions, thin-sliced
1 C chicken broth
1 pkg thawed frozen French-style green beans
1 C drained bean sprouts
1 C sliced bamboo shoots
1 T cornstarch
2 T sherry
½ tsp sugar
4 scallions, minced with green tops
Toasted almond slivers—¼ or ½ C

Prepare everything *first*: sliced, minced, measured or whatever, and line up on the kitchen counter ready to go.

Bone the chicken and cut into matchsticks. Heat the oil with garlic, salt and soy sauce. Sauté chicken 8-10 minutes over medium heat, turning until nicely gilded. Add onions; stir/cook 3 minutes. Add chicken broth, and bring to a boil; reduce slightly, add green beans and bean sprouts to cook 1 minute. Add bamboo shoots, cover and cook 2 minutes. Dissolve cornstarch and sugar in sherry, and thicken the pan sauce; simmer 1 minute, stirring smooth. Serve sprinkled with scallions and toasted almonds (as many as you like).

CINTRA—for 4

Chicken parts for 4
½ stick butter
1 T olive oil

1 peeled pressed garlic clove
6 minced shallots
½ C each: white Port, dry white wine
2 T cherry brandy
¼ C brandy
1 C heavy cream, whipped
2 egg yolks

Brown unfloured chicken parts in butter/oil with garlic and shallots for 20-25 minutes over medium low heat, until completely gilded. Add the wines and brandies, and flame the pan (see METHODS). When flames die, reduce heat to a minimum. Cover and simmer 30-40 minutes until chicken is fork-tender. Remove to a warmed platter.

Whip the cream. Separately beat the egg yolks. Combine cream and yolks, and thicken the pan sauce (see METHODS). Cook 5-10 minutes over lowest heat, stirring constantly. Do not allow a boil. Taste for seasoning; you may want a bit of salt and pepper. Pour sauce over chicken, and serve at once.

POULET BOURBONNAIS—for 6

4 lb chicken parts, assorted to your fancy
6 T butter
2 T olive oil
½ C Bourbon whiskey
1 C each: sliced yellow onions, grated peeled carrots
2 C chopped peeled ripe tomatoes
1½ C heavy cream
1 tsp salt
½ tsp white pepper
1 large can drained pear halves

Brown unfloured chicken in butter/oil for 20-30 minutes

over medium low heat, turning until completely golden. (You may need to do two lots; don't crowd the pan.)

With all browned chicken in the pan, add Bourbon and stir vigorously for 2 minutes over high heat—but do NOT flame! Merely tilt and turn to bathe all pieces in pan juices.

Add everything else but the pears, stirring constantly over high heat until pan juice comes to a boil. Reduce heat sharply to absolute minimum, cover the pan and simmer 30 minutes until chicken is fork tender. Add the drained pears, simmer 1-2 minutes merely to warm through, and serve.

CHICKEN MONTMORENCY—for 4

Chicken parts for 4
¼ C butter
1 T olive oil
¼ tsp salt
1 T flour
1 tsp sugar
⅛ tsp each: cinnamon, allspice
1 lb can of sour pie cherries
1 consommé packet
2 T pineapple juice—if you happen to have it

Brown unfloured chicken parts in butter/oil 20-30 minutes until gilded, and remove temporarily. To the pan, add flour and all seasonings, stirring smooth in the drippings. Slowly pour in the *juice* drained from the tin of cherries and the pineapple juice, if you have it, and stir to a smooth sauce (see METHODS). Add the consommé packet, and stir to dissolve. Return chicken parts, cover and simmer 40 minutes until fork tender. Add the drained cherries, and warm through for a final five minutes.

CHICKEN BENEDICTINE—for 4

Chicken parts for 4
2 T each: butter, olive oil
½ lb quartered fresh mushrooms
¼ C heavy cream
2 T Benedictine
½ tsp salt
¼ tsp pepper

Brown unfloured chicken parts in butter/oil 20-30 minutes over medium heat until nicely gilded. Cover, reduce heat to a minimum and simmer 15 minutes; add the mushrooms, cover and simmer 10 minutes, or until chicken is fork tender. Remove to a warmed serving platter, and discard all but 1 T of the pan drippings. To this, add cream, liqueur, salt and pepper. Stir to blend smoothly over lowest heat for 2-3 minutes without boiling, and pour over the chicken just before serving.

CHICKEN NANTAISE—for 4

Chicken parts for 4
4 T butter
1 T olive oil
½ C dry white wine
½ tsp vinegar
2 small peeled chopped ripe tomatoes
2 small tins tiny boiled onions, drained
½ lb mushrooms, coarse-cut
3 T heavy cream
1 T minced fresh parsley
½ tsp each: salt, pepper, paprika

Brown unfloured chicken parts in butter/oil for 20-30 minutes over medium heat until gilded. Add mushrooms and onions, cover the pan and simmer 10-15 minutes over lowest heat. Drain off all but 1 T of pan drippings, add wine, vinegar, seasonings and tomatoes. Cover and cook 5 minutes or until fork tender. Remove chicken and vegetables to a warmed serving dish. Add cream to the pan sauce, stirring slowly to blend well, and cook over lowest heat for 3 minutes. Strain the sauce over the chicken, top with minced parsley and serve.

CHICKEN COGNAC—for 4

Chicken parts for 4
¼ C butter
1 T olive oil
2 peeled garlic cloves, halved
1 C each: dry white wine, heavy cream
½ C Cognac
2 egg yolks
½ tsp each: salt, pepper
¼ tsp nutmeg

Brown unfloured chicken parts in butter/oil with the garlic over medium heat, 20-30 minutes until gilded. Remove garlic and discard. Add wine and Cognac, flame the pan (see METHODS), shaking the pan vigorously until flames die. Reduce heat to low, cover pan and simmer 20-30 minutes until chicken is fork tender. Remove it to a heated platter. Combine cream with slightly beaten egg yolks, and thicken the pan sauce (see METHODS). Add seasonings, and stir constantly for 5-7 minutes over lowest heat until smoothly thickened without boiling. Pour over the chicken and serve.

CHICKEN MAJORCA—10-12 portions for a sit-down dinner

- 9 lb chicken parts to your choice
- ½ stick butter
- 2 T olive oil
- ½ C Calvados
- 1 T each: meat glaze (Bovril), tomato paste, orange marmalade
- 2 T arrowroot
- 1 C dry white wine
- 2 fresh oranges: grated rind and juice of both
- 2 tsp pepper

Melt butter/oil in a Dutch oven and brown unfloured chicken parts—do two batches, 20-30 minutes each, gilding completely over medium heat. Set all browned parts together in the pan, pour on the Calvados and flame (see METHODS). Reduce the heat when flames die and temporarily remove the chicken. To pan juice, add everything but arrowroot and wine, and stir smooth over low heat for 1-2 minutes. Dissolve the arrowroot in the wine, add to the pot and stir/cook about 5 minutes to thicken the sauce lightly—it should be fairly thin; add 1 T water if necessary.

Replace the chicken, turning to coat with the sauce. Cover the Dutch oven and bake 45 minutes at 375. Remove the cover. At this point, depending on whether you are ready to serve, you may lower the heat to 250 and continue to bake (uncovered) for 30-40 minutes . . . OR you can raise the heat to 425 for 10-15 minutes to brown the chicken lightly.

CHICKEN NABOB—for 8-10

8 lb frying chickens—buy whole carcasses
2 large cans pineapple chunks—drain and reserve juice
2 C chicken stock
2 T cornstarch
1½ T soy sauce
⅛ tsp ground ginger
½ tsp cinnamon
1 C chopped blanched almonds
1 C raisins

Wrap the whole chickens (you may need 4 to make the 8 lb) in loose folds of aluminum foil and bake 1 hour at 375, or until fork tender. Unwrap very carefully—preserve every bit of juice in the foil packages and pour into a bowl. Set in the fridge long enough to congeal fat which you skim and discard; if pressed for time, set the bowl in the freezer for 30 minutes. Anyway, get the fat off, and measure the liquid; extend it to 2 C with water and consommé packets.

When cool enough to handle, strip every bit of meat from the chickens and cut in bite-sized pieces. Discard skin and bones—or thriftily set 'em in a stock pot for soup tomorrow.

Combine 2 C pineapple juice, 2 C chicken stock and 2 T cornstarch stirred smooth in a bit of the juice. Heat over medium high flame, stirring until it reaches a simmer. Cook 2 minutes, stirring to thicken smoothly. Add the chicken (you should have 5-6 C) and everything else: pineapple, almonds, raisins, seasonings . . . reduce the heat to minimum, mixing well, and simmer about 10 minutes before transferring to the buffet table.

SQUABS OPORTO—for 6

6 squabs, with giblets
6-8 slices white bread, trimmed
6 chicken livers

2 T butter, melted
1 tsp salt
½ tsp pepper
¼ tsp allspice
6 oz white Port
3 T heavy cream
3 oz chicken stock
½ tsp nutmeg
6-8 T soft butter
2 T currant jelly

Sauté chicken livers and squab giblets in the melted butter, about 10 minutes stirring over medium low heat. Chop fine. Crumble the bread well, and mix with giblets. Add salt, pepper, allspice, cream and 3 T of the Port wine. Mix thoroughly and stuff the squabs. Truss them neatly and smear generously with soft butter. Set in a baking pan with 3 oz white Port, chicken stock and nutmeg. Cover and cook 30 minutes at 375, basting once. Remove the cover, and baste/turn constantly for 15-20 minutes until browned. Remove to serving plates. Deglaze the pan with 2 T additional Port, scraping up all the nice browned bits over low heat for 2-3 minutes. Add currant jelly, allow to melt partway, and serve the sauce in a gravy boat.

CHICKEN AH SO—for 4

2 C leftover cooked chicken
2 egg yolks, beaten light
1½ tsp soy sauce
¼ tsp salt
⅔ C milk (or water)
⅓ C flour
1 large can pitted litchis, with ½ can of juice
¼ C chicken broth
2 tsp cornstarch

½ tsp fresh ginger, grated
1 C oil

Cut the chicken into pieces roughly 2" square—you want small serving pieces, not tiny chunks.

Make a thin batter of eggs, 1 tsp soy, salt, milk and flour, beating free of any lumps. Heat the oil to 350 in an electric frying pan. Coat chicken pieces in batter, and fry about 10 minutes until golden brown on both sides. Drain thoroughly.

Separately combine ½ tsp soy sauce, ginger and litchi juice over low heat. Dissolve cornstarch in broth, and thicken the litchi juice, stirring about 5 minutes over medium low heat. Finally add drained litchis (you should have about 1 C), heat without boiling, and pour over the chicken.

NOTE: Litchis are extremely sweet! Serve with plain steamed rice and green salad in a tart Vinaigrette dressing.

CHICKEN CALICUT—this is versatile

4 T butter
4 T flour
2 C warmed thin cream
1 T each: curry powder, minced drained chutney, grated onion, minced chives
1 tsp Worcestershire
2 T each: chopped almonds, minced peeled tart apple
2 or 2½ C cooked chicken
½ C toasted grated coconut

Make a sauce of butter, flour and cream (see METHODS). When smoothly thickened, add everything but chicken and coconut. Stir to mix well, cover and remove from heat.

Toast the coconut by spreading on a pan and baking 10-15 minutes at 200 until lightly gilded.

NOW: Cut the chicken fairly fine to use for a warm cocktail or late evening dip . . . cut in bite-sized pieces for a buffet entrée. The sauce can be made a day ahead, if you like. Add the chicken and reheat in the chafing dish. The coconut is added at the very last moment, to retain crispness. The above is enough for 10-12 at a cocktail or midnight party—flank it with hot unbuttered toast squares for dipping, making fresh toast in relays to keep it hot. For a buffet dinner, double the recipe and serve with boiled rice.

Meat

Beef is the glamor meat for parties at any hour of the day, of course, but you can do quite a lot with the humbler pork, lamb or veal. Stews are by no means to be despised for luncheons or even the most impressive dinner, although the real masterpiece is always:

BEEF WELLINGTON—for 6-8

> 3 lb whole beef filet, weighed after trimming off the fat
> ¼ C soft butter
> 1 T coarsely ground black-and-white Java pepper
> 2 unpeeled yellow onions
> 3 unpeeled carrots
> 2 stalks of celery
> 2 bay leaves
> ½ tsp rosemary
> ¼ C dry Vermouth
> NO SALT!!
>
> ½ lb finely chopped mushrooms
> 1 minced shallot
> 2 T butter

½ tsp salt
1 tsp minced fresh parsley
2 T minced truffles (highly optional at today's prices!)
1 small tin of foie gras
1 recipe of plain pastry (see below)

Prepare a vegetable bed in a suitable roasting pan (pay attention, because this is the standard way to roast all plain meats): coarse-sliced onions, carrots, washed celery stalks with leaves—*without* peeling. The onion skins darken the pan juice for handsome gravy later on. Distribute about the pan bottom; wipe the filet with paper towels, and hand-coat every inch with the soft butter. Sprinkle on the pepper, and you may want more than 1 T; I usually do, but it's meant to be only a sprinkle all over. Finally set the beef on the vegetables, add bay leaves and rosemary, and pour Vermouth gently around the base.

I repeat in clarion tones of agitation: NO SALT! It will absorb all the juice from your $15 filet.

In my house, filet is only and always served blood-rare. Thus I roast this 25 minutes at 400; you may want another 2-3 minutes, but be wary, because it gets some more cooking later on. Time exactly, remove at once, and cool to room temperature.

In a shallow skillet, melt 2 T butter, add shallot, mushrooms, salt and parsley. Cook/stir frequently over medium low heat until every bit of liquid has boiled away—it will take an hour of leisurely simmer; don't let the mushrooms brown. At this point, you add the minced truffles, if you can afford 'em.

Next make the plain pastry:

2½ C flour
5 tsp sugar
1 scant tsp salt
4 T butter

9 T lard
4-5 T ice water

Sift together flour, salt and sugar. Pastry-cut the cold butter and lard into the flour until it is grainy. Bind with 4 T ice water, collecting the dough into a ball and adding extra water only if needed. Wrap in waxed paper and chill about 30 minutes. On a pastry board roll the dough between 2 lightly floured sheets of waxed paper until it is ⅛" thick, trimming it into a rectangle that will cover the filet.

Spread the trimmed oblong first with the foie gras—a light covering. Top with the cooled mushroom mixture (known as *duxelles*). Set the filet in the middle and fold up the pastry, sealing the ends to encase the beef completely. Set seam-side down in another roasting pan, and paint the top minutely with a beaten egg yolk.

Bake 15 minutes at 450, until lightly browned. Remove and let sit, keeping warm, for 10 minutes before slicing.

Separately, strain off the pan juices from the first baking of the filet; degrease—set in the freezer for 15-20 minutes or until fat congeals on the top, when you skim and discard. Reheat the liquid gently, and extend to 2 C with water and a bouillon packet. Thicken with beurre manié of 1 T each flour mashed with butter (see METHODS). Stir/cook over low heat until smooth for about 10 minutes, and serve in a sauce boat, dribbling a bit decoratively about the *side* of each filet slice on the plates. Do not cloud the glory of the meat in its pastry overcoat!

FONDUE BACCHUS—for 4

2 lb filet mignon, cut in 1" cubes
2 C each: chicken broth, dry white wine
1 thin-sliced peeled white onion
3 celery stalks with leaves, chopped fine

1 peeled minced garlic clove
8 crushed juniper berries
10 peppercorns
½ tsp each: salt, thyme
1 T minced fresh parsley
1 tsp tarragon
1 bay leaf

Combine broth and wine, bring to a boil; add everything but beef cubes, and again bring just to a boil over medium heat. Cool, cover and set in the fridge for 3-4 days. Strain into a saucepan and bring to a boil over high heat. Transfer to the fondue pot over a table warmer, and hold at a simmer.

Apportion the beef cubes among four dinner plates, and proceed as for Fondue Bourguignonne: guests cook their own beef in the hot liquid to their personal taste. Serve with the usual array of dipping sauces: curry mayonnaise, mustard mayonnaise, chili sauce, minced chopped chutney, Chinese plum or duck sauce, etc.

FILET SEVERINE—for 6

6 filets mignons, cut ¾" thick
10 shallots, minced
¾ C butter
½ C of tinned jellied consommé
6 T Armagnac
6 T heavy cream
1 tsp paprika

Melt ¼ C butter and sauté shallots over medium low heat for 10 minutes, stirring until completely soft without browning. Remove from heat, add the jellied consommé, cover and keep warm.

Melt remaining butter in a skillet that will hold *all* the filets. Turn heat high, add steaks and sear swiftly, turning once. Lower heat to medium, and sauté 2-3 minutes on each side. Add the Armagnac and flame the pan (see METHODS). When flames die, lower heat to minimum, add cream, shallots and paprika, stirring for 1 minute. Serve at once.

ROQUEFORT STEAK—for 4

    2½ lb porterhouse steak, cut 1½" thick
    6 T Roquefort
    1 T dry sherry
    ⅓ C Claret or Burgundy
    Kitchen Bouquet and a pastry brush
    Fresh ground black pepper

Blend cheese and sherry to a smooth paste. Make small incisions 2½" apart on both sides of the steak, cutting only halfway through. Pack the cheese paste into the slits; use it all, making more slits if needed. Paint one side of the steak with Kitchen Bouquet (lightly but thoroughly) and broil 3" below heat for 4 minutes.

Sprinkle cooked side of the steak with pepper, turn and paint the other side lightly with Kitchen Bouquet. Broil again for 3-4 minutes. Remove to a warmed platter and sprinkle lightly with more pepper. NO SALT! There's enough in the cheese.

To the broiler pan juices, add Claret or Burgundy. Stir 1-2 minutes over medium heat to warm through, and pour over the steak.

FLANK STEAK ORIENTALE—for 4

    2 lb flank steak
    ⅓ C soy sauce
    ¼ tsp Tabasco
    ⅓ C dry sherry
    2 slices minced fresh ginger
    1 peeled garlic clove cut in half
    1 tsp pepper

Rub the steak with garlic thoroughly, sprinkle with pepper and lay in a shallow pan. Combine everything else, adding the garlic, and pour over the meat. Cover loosely and hold at room temperature for 3-4 hours, turning occasionally.

Drain the steak from the marinade and broil 3-4 minutes on each side. Slice thin across the grain, as for London Broil.

BOEUF BOURGUIGNONNE—for 10-12

    5 lb boneless chuck, cut in 1½" cubes
    ½ C flour
    ¼ C butter
    2 T olive oil
    ¼ tsp pepper
    ½ C brandy
    2½ C Burgundy
    4 peeled minced garlic cloves
    2 C peeled yellow onion, coarse-cut
    2 stalks of celery, coarse-cut

2 scraped carrots, coarse-cut
½ green pepper, seeded and cut in strips
1 tsp each: thyme, salt, pepper, paprika, chervil
2 bay leaves
1 T minced fresh parsley
½ tsp MSG
1 lb fresh mushrooms, sliced
2 T butter

Melt butter/oil in a large Dutch oven. Toss beef cubes in flour with pepper to coat well, and brown a few at a time over fairly high heat: work quickly and thoroughly sear all sides of each cube, removing temporarily. Allow 20-30 minutes, and finally put them all into the kettle once more. Pour over the brandy and flame the pot (see METHODS). When flames die, add everything else but the mushrooms and final butter. Stir to mix well, cover and either bake 2½ hours at 350, or simmer over lowest possible heat for 2½ hours.

Sauté the mushrooms in the 2 T butter, covered over medium low heat for 10-15 minutes, stirring occasionally. Add to the main pot after 2 hours.

If dinner is delayed, remove the pot from direct heat. Let it sit, covered, to be reheated gently for 10-15 minutes before serving.

I like beef stews with a big pot of fluffy mashed potatoes (add 2 healthy dashes of ground mace or allspice for a "different" flavor), and I do not thicken for a gravy. The pot liquor will have a little body from the original searing flour.

Lamb is only for the sit-down dinner party—if then, because lamb does not lend itself to much gussie-up. Certain things go better than others for flavor: Italianate herbs, such as rosemary, thyme, basil, oregano and garlic . . . dill and fennel are nice, but all seasonings for lamb must be in small amounts because lamb has its own very positive taste. It does not respond well to a flambé, aside from a little dark rum for double-thick loin chops to be finished in the oven.

Anybody can roast a lamb leg; what's needed is a meat thermometer to tell when it's done. Otherwise, rub the leg with a cut clove of garlic or insert bits into tiny slits . . . 1 tsp each of two herbs plus some pepper . . . set on a bed of coarse-cut unpeeled vegetables and roast at 325. You can add ¼ C Madeira or Marsala, and baste occasionally. These days most people like lamb pink rather than totally cooked; at 160 on the meat thermometer, slice into the leg and examine—it will probably be just right.

Do not misunderstand—I am very fond of lamb. Simply, I feel it's of limited use in *party* menus. Double thick loin chops, a roasted leg, or shanks carved in the kitchen—that's about IT. Everything else seems informal or family-style to me. Lamb stew, lamb curry, lamb kidneys—all are delicious, but I wouldn't serve them at a buffet.

MARSALA LAMB SHANKS—for 2

  2 lamb shanks
  3 peeled garlic cloves
  2 tsp each: crumbled rosemary, pepper
  4 T each: melted butter, olive oil
  ½ C Marsala

Insert slivers of garlic in tiny cuts all over the lamb shanks. Rub the meat with rosemary and pepper. Set in a roasting pan, pour over butter, oil and wine. Brown 10 minutes at 400, turning frequently to sear all sides. Reduce heat to 325, and roast about 1 hour until fork tender, basting often.

Lamb shanks *must* be carved in the kitchen! They look a bit frightening on a dinner plate, one is not *sure* they may not bite . . . and even a steak knife is not really sharp enough to tackle a lamb shank with éclat. Nevertheless, shanks are the answer for a small quantity of roast lamb, which everyone likes (in moderation). So carve neat slices for each dinner plate, moisten with a little pan juice, and leave the bones out of sight.

GIGOT EN CROÛTE BAUMANIÈRE—for 10-12

    1 boned lamb leg, 4-5 lb net weight
    4 lamb kidneys
    2 T butter
    ½ C minced mushroom stems
    ⅓ C Madeira
    ¼ C soft butter
    2 tsp each: rosemary, thyme, tarragon
    1 tsp pepper
    2 each: yellow onions, carrots, celery stalks with leaves
    Plain pastry

What this IS is Beef Wellington with lamb.

Mince the kidneys, sauté in 2 T butter with mushrooms over medium high heat, turn/toss leisurely for 5-7 minutes. Add Madeira, cover and reduce heat to minimum. Simmer 10 minutes.

Rub the lamb leg inside and out with soft butter and all the herbs. Make a vegetable bed of onions, carrots, celery (unpeeled, coarse-sliced) in a roasting pan. Stuff the lamb leg with the kidney mixture (reserving any excess liquid). Roll up and tie about 2" apart with kitchen string. Set on the vegetables, roast 10 minutes at 450. Reduce heat to 375 for 25 minutes. Remove from oven and cool.

Make the pastry:
2½ C flour
1 tsp each: salt, sugar
¾ C lard
¼ C butter
4-5 T ice water

Cut lard and butter into flour mixed with salt and sugar. When grainy, bind with ice water. Form a ball and chill 20 minutes. Roll between lightly floured sheets of waxed paper to ⅛" thick on a pastry board. Trim to a rectangle to cover the lamb, which you set in the middle. Fold the pastry around it, sealing the ends. Transfer seam-side down to a roasting pan, paint with 1 beaten egg yolk, and roast 30 minutes at 375.

As for Beef Wellington, pour off pan juices and discard the vegetable bed. Combine with any excess kidney cooking juice. Extend what you have with water to make 1½ C, and thicken with 2 tsp cornstarch stirred in 1 T Madeira. Taste carefully. You may want a bit of salt and pepper.

VARIATION: Instead of the kidney stuffing . . .

1 lb finely ground veal
2 egg whites
1 C light cream
2 T each: minced shallot, celery, parsley
1 T minced fresh dill
1 tsp minced peeled garlic
⅛ tsp nutmeg

Combine everything, mixed thoroughly, and stuff a 5-6 lb (net weight) boned lamb leg. Roll up and tie. This time set on a rack in the roasting pan, with 1 C mixed Claret and water beneath. Roast 20 minutes at 375; reduce heat to 350 and roast 1½ hours, basting every 20 minutes with 2 T each wine and water. Finally remove and cool. Wrap in pastry as above, brush with 1 beaten egg yolk mixed with 2 T heavy cream, and roast 25 minutes at 400.

AGNELLO CON LIMONE—for 8-10

5-6 lb leg of lamb
1 fresh lemon
2 tsp pepper
1 large peeled garlic clove
½ C water
3 T butter, melted
½ C chili sauce
2 T Worcestershire
½ C lime marmalade

Rub lamb with cut clove of garlic and pepper; sprinkle over it the lemon juice. Drop the remains of garlic and juiced lemon into the bottom of the roasting pan, together with a vegetable bed of coarse-cut unpeeled onion-carrot-celery stalks. Set the lamb on top, pour water into the bottom among the vegetables, and pour the melted butter over the lamb. Roast 30 minutes at 325. Combine chili sauce and Worcestershire; pour over the lamb and continue roasting, basting often until meat thermometer says 150. Spread the lime marmalade over the top of the lamb, and finish in the oven for 30 minutes at 350.

Again, pork is not really for parties aside from the handsome roast loin or glazed ham—for which you will find recipes in any book. I use honey or maple syrup or brown sugar with a dash of cloves—sometimes I simply baste with

Madeira or Burgundy, and use nutmeg, allspice or cinnamon instead of cloves—depending on how I feel that day. Nobody needs recipes for this, nor directions for a patio barbecue of ribs . . . and somehow ribs done in the oven, no matter how delicious, are not exactly *party* when eaten at table.

RUM LOIN—for 4

>   1 pork loin of 8 chops
>   1 C dark Jamaican rum
>   1 bottle Sauterne
>   3 tart cooking apples

Have the chops cracked for easy carving, brush thoroughly with the rum—get into every crevice—and store in the fridge for at least 6 hours, brushing again with pan juice when you think of it. Cut the apples in quarters and add to the pan; pour over the bottle of Sauterne, wrap loosely in wax paper and store overnight in the fridge, turning often (when you're awake). Finally set the pan in a 325 oven with all marinade juices and apples, and roast until tender by the meat thermometer. Allow about 30 minutes per pound, and baste occasionally with pan juices.

PORK TAIWAN—for 6-8

>   1½ lb ground pork
>   1½ lb fresh green string beans
>   1 C each: sliced water chestnuts, bean sprouts, shredded lettuce
>   ¼ C minced scallions
>   3 T vegetable oil
>   1 minced peeled garlic clove

¾ tsp salt
2 T soy sauce
1 C water
2 tsp cornstarch dissolved in ½ C water

Prepare all the vegetables; reserve lettuce and scallions for serving time. Cut the beans very fine, French-style if you like.

Brown the ground pork in hot oil over medium heat, stirring for 4-5 minutes. Add garlic, salt, soy sauce and water chestnuts; cook 1 minute. Add water, bring to a boil, add fresh beans and bean sprouts. Stir/cook 1 minute. Reduce to absolute simmer, cover and cook 2 minutes. Thicken with the dissolved cornstarch, stirring over low heat for 3-4 minutes.

Line a serving bowl with the shredded lettuce. Pour in the pork mixture and sprinkle with scallions. I like this served with Chinese vermicelli instead of the ubiquitous rice.

CHU JOU CHEJU-DO—for 4

2 lb fresh pork tenderloin, cut in ¾" slices
2 T butter
1 T oil
2 T minced fresh parsley
1 tsp rosemary
1 tsp salt
½ tsp each: nutmeg, pepper
dash of garlic powder
½ C Japanese saki or dry white wine

Trim every bit of fat from the pork, slice and sauté gently in butter/oil over low heat for 10-15 minutes until slices are browned on both sides. Add everything else, cover the pan, reduce to minimum heat and simmer tender for 30 minutes. Stir occasionally, and add a bit of water if needed.

NOTE: My brother brought this home from Korea; unfortunately, he neglected to get precise instructions, but he says this is an edible reproduction. I append the apologia for the benefit of anyone who's visited Cheju-Do . . .

PORC AUX FRUITS—for 6

3 lb fresh pork tenderloin
½ C honey
2 T orange juice
1 dash of ground cloves
1 fresh orange, sectioned
¼ lb prunes
1 C dry white wine (Vouvray or leftover Champagne)

Soak the prunes in wine overnight; simmer tender and pit, reserving marinade.

Combine honey, orange juice and cloves. Paint over the pork and roast as usual: 40-50 minutes at 375, basting often. Pour the prune marinade around the base of the tenderloin and add pitted prunes and orange sections—roast 5 minutes more and serve. *NOTE*: You can use almost any fresh fruits for final 5 minutes: sliced peaches, pears, apples, damson plums. You *always* need the orange, but any dry white wine will suffice for the last tour in the oven. You can marinate your fresh fruits in it for 1-2 hours, if you like.

SOUR CREAM CHOPS—for 4

4 double-thick loin pork chops
1 T each: butter, olive oil
½ tsp each: salt, pepper, paprika

1 C sour cream
4 minced scallions (include some green top)

Have the butcher remove the chine bones of the chops.
Melt butter with oil, and over very low heat brown the
chops on both sides for 7-10 minutes. Discard all grease.
Transfer chops to a casserole, sprinkle with seasonings,
distribute sour cream on top and cover with the minced
scallions. Cover the casserole and bake 40 minutes at 300
until tender.

Veal is a pleasant change for dinner parties. You can have
it stuffed and roasted, or scallopini and cutlets. The boned
shoulder or rump usually serves 8-10 people generously,
and you can use your preferred stuffing, or . . .

VEAU à la GENDARME—for 8-10

4 lb boned veal rump (net weight)
½ C unsalted shelled pistachio nuts
¼ C boiled tongue, cut in matchsticks (¼" square)
2 tsp each: basil, thyme, rosemary
¼ C Port
1 C consommé

Have the butcher cut the boned veal nearly through, so
that it spreads out flat. Soak the herbs in the wine for 20
minutes. Lightly oil the bottom of a roasting pan, and set
the oven for 525.

Now what you are going to DO is to set the pistachio nuts and tongue slivers in rows along the inside of the veal, roll up and tie firmly—so that when you slice crossways for serving, there will be flecks of green and red in each portion. This takes a bit of care, because the nuts and tongue slivers are apt to roll out of position while you are rolling the rump . . . although it doesn't really matter in the final effect if there are two flecks close together and an empty space before the next flecks—I suppose.

Place veal in the pan, and sear on all sides for 20 minutes, turning frequently. Lower oven heat to 300, pour wine and herbs over the meat, add consommé round the base, and insert the meat thermometer. Roast to 170 on the scale, about 2–2½ hours, basting frequently. Add a bit more port, if you like—let your conscience be your guide. Remove from oven and let sit for 20 minutes before slicing.

BOHEMIAN VEAL—for 4

    2 lb scallopini slices
    ½ C flour
    3 T olive oil
    ½ tsp each: salt, garlic powder, paprika, dry mustard
    ¼ tsp each: rosemary, Worcestershire, pepper
    2 T chili sauce
    1 C each: Sauterne, sour cream

Pound the veal very thin, dredge in flour and sear quickly in hot oil over high heat for 1-2 minutes. You may have to do two or three batches; don't crowd the pan. Return all veal slices to the pan, combine everything else but sour cream and pour over the meat. Reduce heat sharply to absolute minimum. Cover and simmer 50 minutes until tender, turning the slices occasionally. Remove them to a

warmed platter, add sour cream to pan juices and stir to
blend well. Heat without boiling for 2-3 minutes, and pour
over meat.

VEAU À L'ORANGE—for 6

    6 veal cutlets
    1 tsp pepper
    ¼ C butter
    1 T olive oil
    2 T minced shallot
    Juices of 1 lemon, 1 orange
    ¼ C Grand Marnier
    2 tsp each: grated fresh rind of 1 lemon, 1 orange
    1 C milk
    2 T flour
    1 C chicken consommé
    8 oz sliced mushrooms
    ¼ C sour cream

Pound the cutlets thin, sprinkling with pepper. Gild in
the butter/oil over high heat, turning swiftly for 1-2 minutes. Transfer to a shallow baking dish, cover with foil,
and bake 20 minutes at 300.

To the skillet juices, add shallot and sauté soft without
browning. Add all the juices and grated rind. Simmer over
lowest heat for 2 minutes, scraping to deglaze the pan. Stir
milk into flour very slowly, stirring to prevent lumps. Add
to the pan and stir/cook over lowest heat until smoothly
thickened. Disregard any curdle! Add consommé and
mushrooms; cover and simmer 5-8 minutes, stirring occasionally. Remove from the heat, stir in the sour cream and
taste for seasoning; you may want some pepper. Pour over
the veal and serve.

VEAL IN ASPIC—luncheon for 6-8

> 1 veal knuckle
> 1 thick section of veal shank
> ½ C each: minced fresh parsley, chopped pitted black
>   olives
> 1 large yellow onion, peeled
> ½ tsp salt
> ¼ tsp pepper
> ¼ C Chablis
> 3 hardboiled eggs

Simmer veal knuckle and shank in water to cover with the onion for 30-40 minutes until meat is very tender. Remove meat from the bones, and return bones to liquid; continue to simmer.

Mince the veal—use a sharp knife, don't grind—combine with parsley, olives and seasoning. Slice the eggs and arrange decoratively in the bottom of a ring mold. Top with the meat mixture, and sprinkle judiciously with the wine to moisten.

Reduce the stock with bones over high heat by half, or to about 1 C. Dribble over the mold, using only enough to moisten the meat and cause it to hang together. Chill in the fridge for several hours. There should be enough natural gelatin in the stock to set firmly. Unmold on a lettuce-lined plate and fill the center of the ring with watercress. Serve with mayonnaise thinned with a bit of light cream.

CÔTELETTE DE VEAU FOYOT—for 4

> 2 lb veal cutlet
> 2 large peeled red onions
> ¼ lb butter

1 celery stalk, minced
¼ of a green pepper, seeded and cut in strips
¼ C mushroom stems, sliced
1 tsp each: salt, paprika
½ tsp each: pepper, MSG
¼ C each: Sauterne, bouillon, grated Parmesan, bread
   crumbs

I usually use a little unseasoned meat tenderizer on the veal, but if your cutlet is more thin and spread out than thick, it's not needed.

Slice one onion into a baking pan and top with the cutlet. Mince the other onion, and sauté with other vegetables in melted butter until the onion is clear and tender (10 minutes over low heat). Stir often and do not allow onion to brown. Mix in the seasonings, and pile the mixture atop the cutlet. Sprinkle with crumbs and grated cheese. Pour wine and bouillon around the base of the meat. Bake uncovered 45 minutes at 375, or until tender, basting every 10-15 minutes.

OISEAUX SANS TÊTES (Veal birds—6 for luncheon)

18 scallopini slices, pounded thin
9 thin slices cold boiled ham, cut in half
3 cloves peeled garlic, pressed
1 tsp rosemary
¼ tsp nutmeg
½ tsp each: salt, pepper
¼ C olive oil
4 raw bacon slices, minced
1 bay leaf
1 C dry white wine
3 T minced fresh parsley
1 large peeled yellow onion, sliced

1 raw scraped carrot, thin sliced
1 stalk minced celery

Top each veal slice with a piece of ham. Combine garlic, rosemary, parsley, nutmeg, salt, pepper and minced celery; spread some of this mixture on the ham, and roll up the meat to a neat package. Tie firmly, tucking in the ends. Brown the rolls in oil over medium heat, turning often to get all sides. Add the minced bacon and cook to render its fat. Add bay leaf and wine, sliced onion and carrot. Cover and simmer over lowest heat until veal is tender, turning the rolls occasionally for about 30-40 minutes. Remove veal to a warmed platter.

Strain pan sauce, and thicken with 2 tsp cornstarch or arrowroot dissolved in 2 T water. Stir/cook over lowest heat for 4-5 minutes, pour over the birds and serve.

NOTE: Veal birds always contain ham—but the seasoning mixture is a matter of invention: it can be bread crumbs mixed with poultry seasoning, or minced sautéed mushrooms, or sautéed shallots with a bit of leftover ground chicken—whatever you happen to have, in fact.

LES OISEAUX FLAMBÉS—for 4

12 scallopini slices
12 thin slices Westphalian ham
1½ tsp pepper
½ C butter
1 T olive oil
¼ C each: Marsala, vodka
1 lb sliced fresh mushrooms
2 T flour
⅔ C heavy cream
2 T minced parsley
2 T Cognac

Trim any really excess fat from the ham and set one slice on each scallopini slice. Sprinkle with the pepper and roll up. Tie neatly with kitchen string or thread on fine metal skewers. Melt ¼ C butter with oil, and brown the veal rolls quickly over high heat for 1-2 minutes, turning to sear all sides. Add Marsala and vodka, flame the pan (see METHODS). When flames die, reduce sharply to simmer. Separately, melt remaining butter and sauté mushrooms with a bit of salt and pepper for 3 minutes over low heat. Sprinkle with the flour, stirring to blend and cook for 2-3 minutes. Slowly add the cream and stir until smoothly thickened (see METHODS). Combine both pans, add parsley and Cognac, and simmer covered for 5 minutes until veal is tender.

Buffet Specialties: "The Big Dish"

Now we come to the Big Dishes: recipes for twelve to twenty or more at a buffet dinner. These will take more preparation time, but much of it can be done yesterday, and most are sufficiently all-encompassing to be the single presentation of the evening. That is, they require only salad and rolls, perhaps some rice, to complete the meal. Some are meat, some are fish, but all are combinations that can't really be placed in previous chapters. Of these, the most useful of all is . . .

SWEDISH MEATBALLS

    6 slices white bread
    1 C milk
    6 T peeled chopped yellow onion
    6 T butter
    2 eggs lightly beaten
    1 lb ground beef (chuck is preferable)

⅓ lb each: ground veal, ground pork
3 T minced fresh parsley
1 T each: salt, Worcestershire
½ tsp pepper
¼ tsp dry mustard
¼ C each: butter, flour
2 C sour cream

Soak bread in milk, while you sauté onion in 6 T butter for 3-4 minutes over medium low heat until it is limp without browning. Squeeze the excess milk from the bread; discard milk and add bread to all other ingredients but the final butter, flour and sour cream.

Work with your hands, and mix for *a full five minutes by the kitchen timer*! This is a nuisancy job, but essential to create the proper texture. Form the meat mixture into 48 small balls for a buffet entrée—60 smaller balls for a cocktail party. Lay them on a baking sheet lined with waxed paper, in layers with waxed paper between and more folded loosely over the top. Chill overnight in the fridge.

To cook: bring out the meatballs to warm for 1 hour at room temperature. Melt the ¼ C of butter in a large skillet; dust the meat balls with the flour, and sauté gently for 15 minutes. Turn constantly to brown all sides, using medium low heat. Do not crowd the pan! Take your time over the cooking: you want the meatballs firm enough on the outside to hold their shape. You will have to do several batches. As finished, remove to a chafing dish and keep warm over hot water. When all are completed, pour over the sour cream. Cover the chafing dish and let it stand for 5 minutes before transferring to the buffet. The cream will curdle—it's supposed to.

You can dust lightly with paprika, if you want . . .

NOTE: Cocktail meatballs require a box of sturdy toothpicks, and omit the sour cream in favor of other dipping sauces, if you like. For the entrée, better serve it yourself to be sure it goes around: 3 apiece for 16 guests, or 2 each for 24 people.

This is THE major mainstay dish for any large party! It is essential for a smorgasbord table, it is the easiest hot cocktail goodie, or sufficient for the single entrée, but teams happily with whatever else you have, such as sliced turkey or cold shrimp salad. Furthermore, there are all sorts of things you can do with your meatballs to delude the guests into thinking it's a new dish!

À LA BACCHUS

   1 batch of Swedish meatballs (48)
   ½ C dark Jamaican rum
   2-3 T Burgundy

Prepare the meatballs through the final sauté operation. When all are browned, return them to the pan and flame with the rum (see METHODS). Bathe the meatballs thoroughly, and when flames die, add the Burgundy. Blend gently into pan sauce, cover and set aside to ripen for 5 minutes. Transfer to the chafing dish or the electric frying pan turned to Warm on the buffet table.

KEFTIDES

   1 recipe of Swedish meatballs (48)
   8 oz tomato sauce
   1 C water
   10 oz grape jelly

For this one, you do not cook the meatballs—merely bring them to room temperature.

Combine tomato sauce, water and jelly. Simmer over low

heat to blend for about 5 minutes. Add the unfloured meatballs, cover the pan and hold at an absolute simmer for 45-60 minutes, turning occasionally. Transfer to chafing dish or electric frying pan for the buffet.

SWEET-AND-SOUR

1 recipe of Swedish meatballs (48)
3 C mixed vegetables and fruits (see below)

Sauce:

6 T cornstarch
2 T soy sauce
6 T white vinegar
1 C sugar
2 C fruit juice (see below)
¾ C water

Dissolve cornstarch in soy and vinegar, stirring smooth. Heat fruit juice with sugar until dissolved, over medium low heat. Add cornstarch mixture and stir over low heat for 15 minutes, thinning slowly with the water until the sauce is smoothly thickened.

Prepare the meatballs and sauté to brown completely; omit sour cream. You can do all of this hours ahead of time, if you like, and simply hold everything at room temperature.

The last minute chore is a swift stir/fry of mixed fruits and vegetables—and these depend on what you happen to have, aside from a large yellow onion; that is essential.

1 large yellow onion, peeled and sliced thin
3 T vegetable oil

To this you add any or all of the following (and from the fruits, you reserve the juice needed for the sauce!)

½ stalk celery, sliced thin
½ scraped carrot, sliced thin
¼ green pepper, seeded and cut in fine strips
1 tart cooking apple, peeled, cored and sliced
1 small can pineapple chunks (reserve the juice!)
2 red radishes, sliced thin
1 small firm tomato, peeled and cut in wedges
1 fresh firm peeled pitted peach, nectarine, apricot
    and/or plum
Seedless white grapes
Blanched cauliflower florets
Mushrooms, cut Chinese fashion
1 small peeled seeded cucumber, sliced ½" thick
3-4 sweet small gherkins, sliced
A few maraschino cherries

Compose 3 C out of the above, keeping the onion to itself. Understand: you do not need ALL—merely a mixture of three or four fruits and vegetables! If there's not enough juice from your fruits, extend with a bit of orange juice and water for the sauce. This 3 C mixture can (should) also be done well in advance; it takes a lot longer to prepare than you'd think.

To cook: heat the oil, sauté onion slices 3 minutes over medium high heat, stirring constantly until slightly softened. Add your 3 C assortment, and continue to stir briskly over medium-high heat for 5 minutes—NO MORE! Scoop out, and drain thoroughly on paper towels.

For the final assembly, set the meatballs in the chafing dish over simmering water . . . heat the sauce, stirring smooth over lowest flame while the vegetables/fruits are draining . . . combine sauce with vegetables/fruits, and pour over the meatballs. Heat 5-10 minutes in the chafing dish, covered, and serve.

NOTE: Sweet-and-Sour is only suitable for an entrée, but both Keftides and Bacchus could be used for a fancy cocktail party—merely make the meatballs smaller.

TIKIA—for a cocktail or large after-dinner party

> 1 recipe of Swedish meatballs (60)
> 8 oz Dijon mustard
> 16 oz currant jelly

Combine mustard and jelly, stirring in the electric frying pan over lowest heat until well blended.

Prepare the meatballs up through the sauté operation, transferring to the sauce as you finish browning them in the kitchen skillet. Cover the electric frying pan and hold over lowest heat for 15-20 minutes before serving—with toothpicks to spear the balls.

MITITE—for a small cocktail party, using the sauce for Tikia

> ½ lb ground chuck
> 1 T minced yellow onion
> ½ T vegetable oil
> ½ tsp salt
> ¼ tsp each: ground cumin, ground coriander
> ⅛ tsp each: cinnamon, cayenne
> ¼ C butter
> Flour to dredge

Combine beef with all seasonings, working together very thoroughly. Form small balls or tiny sausage shapes (2" long). Set on a baking sheet covered with waxed paper and chill several hours in the fridge. Bring to room temperature for 30 minutes, and dust with flour; sauté in melted butter, browning all sides completely over medium low heat for 10-12 minutes.

Use only 4 oz Dijon mustard and 8 oz currant (or tart grape) jelly for the sauce—you won't have as many servings as with Tikia. Transfer everything to the electric frying pan over lowest heat, and serve with toothpicks.

ARROZ CON MARISCOS CON POLLO—for 14-16

4 thawed lobster tails, sliced (shell and all) ¾" thick
1½ lb raw cleaned shrimp—medium to large size
1 lb fresh crab lumps
1½ lb each: mussels, Cherrystone clams
1 large whole chicken breast, boned and cut bite-size
3 chicken thighs, boned and cut bite-size
¼ lb lean pork, diced
6 peeled garlic cloves
2 pimientos, drained and diced
2 large peeled yellow onions, sliced
1 C dry white wine
3½ C raw rice
1 tsp saffron
3 tsp salt
¼ C minced fresh parsley
7 C boiling water (partly fish liquid—read directions)
½ C olive oil (plus a bit more)
2 squid cut in thin rings (optional)

At the outset, this is NOT a recipe to attempt in a kitchenette or if any other part of the menu will require attention beyond transferring from fridge to buffet!

First prepare everything and set in separate covered

dishes: bone and dice the chicken . . . clean the shrimp . . . slice the lobster tails with the kitchen cleaver . . . gently pick over the crab lumps for whatever bits of shell you can find . . . dice the raw pork . . . set the clams and mussels to soak in cold water . . . peel the garlic . . . peel and slice the onion . . . drain and dice the pimiento . . . measure the rice, the olive oil, the saffron . . . mince the parsley and cut the squid in rings ½" thick (and do use it if you can get it).

This will take about an hour—and you must still clean the mussels and clams. Scrub them well with a stiff brush, changing the water often—the clams will be easier than the mussels, which must be debearded ruthlessly (use the pliers from the household tool kit!) When you've got 'em as clean as you think you can, leave them to soak in more fresh cold water and get out two *large* frying pans.

In one, heat ¼ C olive oil with 3 minced garlic cloves. Add the chicken, and sauté over low heat for 20-30 minutes; cover the pan, but stir often until tender. Scoop out with a slot spoon, draining well, and hold the chicken covered at room temperature.

In the other, heat ¼ C olive oil with 3 *whole* garlic cloves, and sauté pork dice for 10-15 minutes, stirring over very low heat until completely tender. Remove the garlic and discard. Add sliced onion, and cook about 5 minutes until onion is limp. Add squid and lobster; stir/cook until the lobster shell reddens. Add the shrimp; stir/cook until slightly pinkened. Add the pimiento, cover the pan and let it sit off heat.

Thus far you can go early in the day, which will clear away a number of the preparation dishes—oh, joy! Twenty minutes before you mean to dress for your party, transfer clams and mussels to a large deep pot with the wine, and steam open (covered over medium high heat) for 10 minutes. Do not shell. Transfer to a pan and hold at room temperature. Strain the cooking liquor through double folds of dampened cheesecloth or dish towel, removing all the sand you can—do it twice, if necessary. Measure the liquid, and add water to make 7 C; use 2-3 T to soak the saffron.

NOW you can tidy the kitchen and go put on your face. All that is left is the final assembly, which will take 35-45 minutes, and not all of it will require supervision. You can serve the first round of drinks, start the guests on appetizers, and then fade away to the kitchen—where you turn the oven to 200 and set the pan of mussels/clams to warm.

Gently reheat both the large skillets, stirring the contents. Leave the chicken pan covered over lowest possible heat. When the lobster pan is heated through, add 2 T olive oil plus the rice, and stir over medium high heat until the rice is well coated with oil and begins to gild. Pour over the 7 C of liquid (including saffron in its soak water), stir briskly and raise heat to bring it to the boil; reduce heat to absolute minimum, cover the pan and let it sit for 20 minutes—don't peek! Remove from the heat, add the crab lumps and contents of chicken pan. Sprinkle with the parsley. Set uncovered in the 200 oven for 15-20 minutes. Transfer tenderly to buffet serving dishes, top with the unshelled clams and mussels . . . and serve.

NOTE: Nearly all these buffet specialties take more time to describe than to do! I will agree that this one is a bit fussy at the end, and will finalize more easily if you have someone to help—whether in the kitchen, or dressing the front of the house while you are stirring and warming things. The end product is a kind of Paella, but all you need for accompaniment is plenty of green salad, rolls and a simple fruit dessert.

BOLLITO MISTO—for 16-20

This is another long description, although much easier than the Arroz, because once it is started, it will do itself with a minimum of attention. It does require special equipment: an immense old-fashioned soup or jelly-making kettle—or two *deep* Dutch ovens . . . a bolt of kitchen cheesecloth, a ball of kitchen string, and some trussing skewers.

1 old hen, 5½-6 lb for fricasee—not disjointed
Stuffing for old hen
1 *fresh* beef tongue, 4-5 lb
1 boned rolled chuck or rump pot roast—6 lb
1 boned rolled shoulder of veal—4 lb
1 large smoked Polish sausage (Kielbasa) or 10 chorizos
12 leeks
1 large bunch of carrots
1 lb yellow onions
2 lb rutabagas
1 large green cabbage
3 T salt
a bouquet garni: 5 peeled garlic cloves, 2 bay leaves, 1 tsp thyme, 6 peppercorns, 4 sprigs fresh parsley—all tied in a bit of cheesecloth

NOW: what you are going to *do* is to cook all these meats and the hen, together with vegetables, until everything is tender—when you will serve a bit of all components accompanied by at least 3 (preferably 5 or 6) different sauces.

The first step is stuffing the chicken, and since it is to be simmered tender, I like a very dry bread stuffing.

2 C dry bread cubes, or commercial stuffing
2 thin-sliced peeled yellow onions
¼ C each: melted butter, minced celery
½ tsp each: thyme, basil, marjoram
2 T brandy

Mix all the dry ingredients with onion—and if you're

using seasoned commercial stuffing, still add my herbs, because the packaged stuff is principally sage which doesn't conflict. Add the melted butter, brandy and celery; toss lightly to mix. Stuff the chicken, close the vent with skewers laced with string, and truss the bird into a neat package—*leaving a 2-foot length of string trailing from the legs!*

Next you attack the vegetables: peel the onions and leave them whole . . . scrape the carrots and cut lengthwise in quarters; if very long, cut in half crossways. Clean the leeks, cut in quarters lengthwise and soak well in cold water. Peel the rutabagas and cut in quarters. Cut the cabbage into large wedges—4 or 6, depending on how big a cabbage you bought (the bigger, the better)—and soak in cold water. Finally, tie each of the drained vegetables into a separate bundle of cheesecloth—leaving a 2-foot length of string on each!

Similarly, wrap the tongue, pot roast and veal in separate bundles of cheesecloth, tying tightly at the top with that 2-foot length of string on each one! Leave the sausage aside, it goes in later. Prepare the bouquet garni—and if you are going to need two kettles for cooking, you will need 2 bouquets garnis.

All of this can be done yesterday and held in the fridge overnight. You start cooking 6 hours before you mean to serve.

Set the chicken and carrot bundle in one kettle with a bouquet garni and 3 T salt . . . set all the other bundles, second bouquet garni and another 3 T of salt in the other kettle . . . and tie all the long strings to the handles outside. Not everything will get done at the same time and you will occasionally have to check on the status. When something is definitely *done,* you must hoick it out to a side plate before it goes to mush.

Cover everything with cold water—I'm assuming you are using two pots because I have to; who has room for a jelly kettle in an apartment? Cover the pots and bring to a boil over high heat. Reduce sharply to absolute minimum, checking the boil with ¼ C cold water. Subsequently simmer covered for 5 hours, checking occasionally to control any illicit boil; everything must *simmer*. After 4 hours, begin testing the various bundles and remove anything that is really done. The vegetables will be first, of course. Half an hour before the last meat will finish (it will be the beef), add the Kielbasa or chorizos.

You are now at 5 hours of simmering. Briefly replace everything to heat through over minimum heat for about 4-5 minutes. Then remove pots to sit covered off heat for 15-20 minutes.

Finally, unpack everything onto an immense platter (if you have one) or onto suitable warmed serving dishes. Do the meats first; they will be easier to carve if they've rested 15-20 minutes. It will take 10 minutes merely to haul them out, drain well, remove cheesecloth, strings and skewers. It will take another 10 minutes to drain out the vegetables and strip off their cheesecloth kimonos. Furthermore, they will be extremely soft and require delicate handling. The carrots, leeks and cabbage should survive recognizably, to be placed in separate piles about the meat platter. The onions may have disintegrated so untidily that they can only be returned to the stock pot. The rutabagas are to be mashed with 2-3 T of butter, a bit of salt and pepper, and piled among the other vegetables.

The final requisite is razor-sharp carving knives: 1 large for the veal and beef, 1 medium-sized for the chicken, tongue and sausage. You will need a spoon to scoop out the chicken stuffing, and other spoons for the vegetables. Theoretically, everyone gets a bit of all the meats, chicken, stuffing and vegetables on his plate. He helps himself to the sauces he fancies—and for this service, you may use bottled commercial sauces.

There can be mustard (Dijon, Düsseldorf, Bahamian, or a fancy bottled variety), tomato (ketchup, chili sauce or

Sauce Robert), a thick meat sauce (A-1, Escoffier or Diablo), curry and/or wine mayonnaise, Béarnaise or Hollandaise (if you've the energy to hot it up). You can have sour cream plain or mixed with minced chives . . . Chinese Duck or Plum Sauce . . . any of the jam-consistency chutneys. You will NOT have a thickened gravy! If you wish, you may strain a bit of the pot liquors and use a single tablespoon to moisten each plate.

I will simplify the whole thing: call it *cucido, puchero, pot au feu* or Kentucky Burgoo (the American version), all that's required is to simmer a combination of meats, poultry, and/or game, with suitable vegetables until tender. The pot liquor is then reserved for soup; the ingredients are drained and served separately, as a sort of road-company smorgasbord.

You don't *have* to use the particular components I've listed—you *could* use some delicious fresh rabbit or squirrel instead of the chicken, or half a ham to replace sausages (if so, omit salt in that pot). If fresh beef tongue isn't available, substitute 4-5 lb of small calves tongues. You can add a cheesecloth bundle of fresh green or wax beans, or use peeled potatoes instead of the turnips (if so, add that bundle only 20-30 minutes before the end, or they'll cook down to smoosh).

ASOPAO—for 10-12

> 4 whole chicken breasts
> 2 slices salt pork, ½" thick
> 1½ C sliced peeled yellow onion
> 1 seeded green pepper, cut in fine strips
> 1 bay leaf
> 8 oz tomato sauce
> ¼ C olive oil
> 2 C chicken broth

1 tsp salt
½ tsp pepper
2 C raw rice
1 lb crab lumps
½ lb cooked cleaned shrimp
2 thin-sliced pimientos
½ C each: drained capers, sliced stuffed green olives
1 pkg frozen asparagus, cooked crisp-tender
½ C tinned petits pois, drained (or a frozen pkg steamed)

Bone the chicken breasts and cut the meat into 1″ cubes. Cook and clean the shrimp. Fine-chop the salt pork, and cook with onion and green pepper over very low heat for 15 minutes, stirring. Add bay leaf and tomato sauce; cook 15 minutes.

In a Dutch oven, heat olive oil and lightly brown the chicken cubes over medium heat, stirring leisurely. To this, add the tomato mixture, chicken broth, salt and pepper. Cover and simmer over lowest heat for 10 minutes. Add the rice, and cook 30 minutes covered over medium low heat, stirring often. Add everything but peas and asparagus; cover and simmer over lowest heat for 5 minutes. Separately, steam/cook peas and asparagus until crisp-tender for about 10 minutes.

Serve the stew in deep soup plates, garnished with the vegetables and flanked with lots of crisp French bread.

PILAU FROM THE WOMAN IN THE NEXT SEAT—for 8-10

I acquired this on the air shuttle to Washington. I wish I could give proper credit, but all I know is that her brother was a Baptist bishop, and the whole family annually awaited her coming to make this dish.

1 roasting chicken, 4-5 lb—truss it unstuffed
¼ C olive oil
2 C sliced peeled yellow onions
2 bottles of clam juice
1 can minced clams with juice (10½ oz)
2 bouillon packets
1 lb each: crab lumps, lobster tails, raw cleaned shrimp
1 C pitted ripe olives
1 pkg thawed artichoke hearts
3 C raw rice
1 tsp saffron, soaked in 1 T water for 20 minutes
5 C water

Brown the trussed chicken in hot oil on all sides over medium low heat, using a deep Dutch oven and turning constantly. Remove and keep warm; in the pot, sauté onions about 5 minutes until limp. Scoop out the onions briefly, set the chicken back in the Dutch oven and put onions on top. Add clams and clam juice with bouillon packets, stirring to dissolve. Cover and hold at an absolute simmer for 1–1½ hours until the chicken is *nearly* fork tender. Add shrimp, lobster, olives and artichokes; cover and simmer 8-10 minutes until shellfish is cooked (oops, forgot! Thaw and shell lobster tails—cut in ¾" slices). Add the crab lumps, and taste the broth for seasoning; you may want some pepper, rarely need salt because of clam juice. Cover again and simmer 5 minutes.

Separately, about 10 minutes before you'll add shellfish to the main pot, bring 5 C water to a full rolling boil with 1 tsp salt—add the rice and strained saffron water. Use a good-sized pot! Let the water boil furiously until it begins to froth up toward the top. Then reduce heat to absolute minimum, cover the pot and let it sit for 20-30 minutes without peeking, until all water is absorbed. Eventually remove from heat and keep warm. I usually set the pot in a 200 oven until ready to serve.

When the chicken is very tender, fish it out and dissect into serving portions, discarding as many bones as possible. Set in a large tureen, and gently pour in the rest of the shellfish broth. The rice is served from a separate large warmed bowl: use old-fashioned soup plates, put some rice in the bottom, and ladle over the soup/stew.

This is a party dish, *yes!*—but it's for family and intimates, because there will be second—even third—helpings. It goes with lots of hot biscuits and green salad.

BAHMI GORENG—for 8-10

1½ lb boneless pork, cut in matchsticks
1 C soy sauce
½ lb vermicelli
2 well-beaten eggs
1 T butter
¾ C vegetable oil
1½ C peeled yellow onion slices
2 peeled garlic cloves, pressed
2 tsp minced fresh ginger
3 C shredded bok choy or Chinese cabbage
1 C drained bean sprouts
1 lb cooked cleaned shrimp, coarse-cut
¼ C chopped scallions (with some of the green tops)
½ tsp pepper

Prepare everything, line it up, ready-set-to-go!

Refrigerate the pork in soy sauce overnight, turning when you think of it. Cook vermicelli *al dente* (10 minutes in boiling salted water); drain and cool on a flat surface; chill two hours. Make an omelette of the eggs in butter—use a fairly large pan and cook the mixture rather thin; roll up any old way, cool and slice in ribbons.

The final assembly takes 20-25 minutes. Scoop the pork

out of the soy marinade (reserving it) and sauté in 2 T oil for 10 minutes over medium heat, stirring often; remove and keep warm. Add 2 T oil to the pan, plus onion, garlic and ginger, and stir/cook for 3 minutes. Remove to join the pork keeping warm. Add 2 T oil to the pan and sauté shredded bok choy (or Chinese cabbage) with the bean sprouts for 3 minutes. Add diced cooked shrimp and sauté 2 minutes. Return everything to the pan, with scallions, pepper, and 1 T of the soy sauce marinade. Stir/cook 2 minutes over medium low heat.

Separately, in a good-sized skillet, heat remaining oil and fry the vermicelli over high heat for 4-5 minutes until nicely browned; drain, add to the pork pan. Finally, turn everything into a large tureen for serving, and sprinkle the sliced omelet on top.

CASSOULET DO BRASIL—for 10

2 lb black beans
1 lb smoked pork spareribs
1 lb smoked ham hocks
½ lb smoked tongue
½ lb salt pork
12 pork sausages, cut in pieces
1 grated peeled white onion
3 peeled garlic cloves, pressed
½ C minced fresh parsley
2 T lard

In separate pots, soak overnight in water to cover: beans, tongue, spareribs, ham hocks.

In the morning, cook the beans in their soak water; drain all the meats and set in a deep stew pot. Cover with fresh water, add the salt pork and simmer 2 hours until tender. Haul out the tongue and skin it—you will obviously have to have a whole tongue to begin with, which will leave you with one or two pounds of cooked meat not needed for the cassoulet, but I never have any trouble in using up tongue. If you do, substitute ½ lb of smoked turkey slices, which do not need to be soaked.

When the smoked meats are tender, cut them into serving pieces and discard bones. Add to the main bean pot and continue to simmer, adding water if needed. When beans are almost tender, add the sliced pork sausages.

Separately, melt the lard and sauté onion, garlic and parsley for 2-3 minutes. Add this to the bean pot and mix well. Simmer 10 minutes more until the beans are thickish—you can't really overcook a cassoulet, it will hold at a simmer for 30-60 minutes. Serve in deep soup plates, garnished with *cold* peeled orange slices, and flanked with green salad containing ripe tomato wedges.

TEMPURA—for 6

This is to be cooked at the table in an electric frying pan with 1½" vegetable oil heated to 400. The way to do it is to have everything prepared in separate dishes. You then dip one item at a time into the batter, drain slightly, and fry for about 3 minutes . . . scoop out, drain on paper towel, and apportion 1 piece for each plate. While everybody is happily wolfing down the first titbit, you rapidly do another that is different . . . and so on, until all the guests have a new taste thrill with each service. Eventually, all the components will have been served in relays, and the cook can sit down to consume his own portion, while everyone else is burping genteelly.

Each guest must have an individual bowl of hot plain rice, and a bowl of dipping sauce. Warmed *saki* is at your discretion, as also the particular ingredients you choose to serve. Select 4-5 items from the following for 6 guests, and expand to your fancy—but you should always have the shrimp and eggplant.

>1 lb large raw cleaned shrimp
>½ medium eggplant, unpeeled, cut ½" thick
>1 large yellow onion, peeled, cut ½" thick
>1 fresh green pepper, seeded and cut in 6 pieces
>2 thawed lobster tails, shelled and cut in ½" slices
>12 Cherrystone clams, steamed open and shelled (or a drained ½ C of minced canned clams)
>1 pkg thawed frozen cauliflower, separated into florets
>1 pkg thawed frozen asparagus tips (use only 2" of each spear)
>1 peeled seeded cucumber, cut in 6 hunks
>12 large fresh spinach leaves, stems off
>12 bay scallops

Understand: you *always* have the shrimp and eggplant . . . but the rest is up to you. Pick whatever you like, and you can prepare everything well in advance—aside from the eggplant; slice it just before cooking or it will discolor in the air. Set thawed vegetables and cucumber hunks on a towel to absorb as much moisture as possible; pat dry because the batter will cling better. If you use drained minced clams, mix them with some batter in a separate dish, and use a slot spoon to transfer to the hot oil.

Batter:

>1 egg yolk
>¾ C water
>½ tsp salt
>¾ C sifted flour

Beat egg yolk with a fork, mix with water. Add salt and flour, stirring thoroughly—but do not try to remove any lumps. The batter should be made at the last moment before starting to cook; do not let it sit. It is supposed to be very thin.

Sauce:

> ¼ C soy sauce
> 1 T dry white wine
> ½ C water
> 1 tsp sugar
> ½ tsp ground ginger
> 3 minced scallions

Mix everything but scallions, and warm gently without boiling. Apportion among six dipping dishes, and sprinkle in the scallions if liked.

MÉLANGE SUPRÊME—for 14-16

> 8 lb chicken parts (see note below)
> ½ C flour
> 1 tsp each: salt, pepper, paprika, basil
> ¼ C each: butter, olive oil
> 3 peeled yellow onions, thin-sliced
> 3 garlic cloves, peeled and pressed
> 2 T minced fresh parsley
> 1 lb sliced fresh mushrooms
> ⅓ C dry sherry
> 2 lb small Cherrystone clams (or 2 cans minced clams)
> 1½ lb raw cleaned shrimp
> 1 small can tomato sauce
> 1 large can tomato purée

For the chicken parts, what's wanted are the smaller pieces, so everybody gets some. You can use chicken breasts, boned and cut into 2" hunks. I generally get small drumsticks and the biceps portion of chicken wings—if necessary buy whole wings and cut apart at home; the bony sections go into soup, or will produce enough meat for grinding to make a canapé spread.

Scrub the clams well and steam open in a ½ C water for 8-10 minutes. Shell and coarse-chop the clams; strain the liquor carefully and reserve (or if you use tinned clams, save the juice).

Add seasonings to flour, dredge chicken parts and lightly gild in melted butter/oil—you will need to do several batches. Transfer to a large deep casserole or baking pan —it must be big enough to take all the rest of the ingredients without overflowing into the oven. Use the roaster, if you have to, and transfer later to the buffet servers.

When chicken is browned, combine garlic and onions in pan fat over low heat, stirring until onions are limp. Add everything else but shrimp, and simmer 10-15 minutes, stirring occasionally. Pour over the chicken, cover and bake 1 hour at 350. Uncover and add the shrimp, pushing them down beneath the sauce. Bake 10-15 minutes, and serve with plain boiled rice.

RAPSODIA DE COSTA DEMONIO—for 12-14

    1 lb ground chuck
    6 fillets of sole, cut in 2" pieces
    3 T butter
    12 each: raw cleaned jumbo shrimp, raw cleaned
        Spanish shrimp
    3 lobster tails, shelled and sliced ¾" thick
    ¼ lb crab lumps
    3 squid, cut in ½" rings
    1 lb mushrooms, halved
    ½ C olive oil
    4-5 peeled ripe tomatoes—purée in the blender to
        make ¾ C

1 large peeled yellow onion, coarse-chopped
2 peeled garlic cloves, pressed
1 lb mussels
¼ lb blanched toasted hazelnuts, coarse-ground
½ tsp each: salt, white pepper
1 C water
½ C dry white wine
½ C minced scallions
2 T minced parsley
1 T flour
1 T Anisette

Scrub and debeard the mussels; open them raw and strain all the juice to remove every bit of sand.

Combine beef, scallions and parsley, mixing well. Heat 2 T oil in a deep Dutch oven and quickly brown the meat over medium high heat. Toss/turn for 5-8 minutes, crumbling as for a spaghetti meat sauce. Spread it evenly over the bottom of the pot and set aside.

Separately, melt butter with remaining olive oil, and sauté fillet of sole pieces unfloured for 5-6 minutes over medium low heat, turning once. When lightly gilded, transfer tenderly atop the browned meat.

In the pan fat, sauté onion until limp; add mushrooms with salt and pepper. Stir/cook over medium low heat for 4-5 minutes. Sprinkle with the flour and stir briskly until absorbed into pan juice. Add tomato purée, and stir for 1 minute. Add the squid rings; cook 7 minutes over medium-high heat, basting with the pan sauce. Add the strained mussel liquor, water, lobster and all the shrimps. Cook 2 minutes; add mussels and hazelnuts, plus white wine. Stir leisurely, to prevent sticking, for about 5-7 minutes. Taste the sauce and add salt or pepper if needed. Gently stir in the crab lumps, and pour the whole thing over browned meat and fish fillets.

Bake uncovered 20-25 minutes at 350. Remove from heat, transfer to the buffet and sprinkle with the liqueur. If you dislike Anisette, use Pernod—to be authentic, it ought to be Absinthe, and if you have a bottle left from before it was outlawed, this is a good way to use it up. That single tablespoon will not make your guests' brains any softer than they already are.

NOTE: Spanish shrimp are those glamorous red-shelled ones—they do have a different taste, but if you can't get them, use 24 plain old American shrimp. Or, on the Pacific coast, use 1 lb of the cooked baby shrimp: set half in a layer atop the sole and add the rest to the sauce at the same time as the crab lumps.

I said these were the buffet *specialités*, and so they are, but mostly these are the few fussy expensive dishes. Some are best served at a table where guests can have knives as well as forks, but all *can* be used for the plate-in-hand party, provided you cut meats or fish into bite-sized pieces. It is even *possible* to present Tempura for a dozen or more guests—you need two electric frying pans, a double supply of batter and two people to cook, with an array of sauces to be spooned onto the guests' plates. Keep the rice covered over hot water and let them take it one spoonful at a time onto their plates, so it's always hot. Frankly, I think it's all more trouble than it is worth, but there is no denying it is impressive if you can manage it.

Vegetables

In general it is best to present a casserole vegetable dish for the large buffet, and rely upon the salads to round out the menu. I fear this chapter will be spotty—nearly all my "different" vegetable recipes were in *Simple Gourmet Cookery*. On the other hand, vegetables are best plain and adorned only with butter, for which no one needs directions. For the festive touch, experiment with a dash of spice or herb in the butter; ⅛ tsp will be enough. Toasted sesame seeds or almond slivers, seasoned stuffing crumbs, a few sliced water chestnuts will add a bit of crunch for all green vegetables. Grated fresh lemon rind is a pleasant change, too—1 tsp is enough.

ARTICHOKES GRANADINA—for 10-12

> 2 peeled yellow onions, chopped
> 3 scraped carrots, coarse-grated
> 5 T olive oil
> 1½ T flour
> 1 tsp salt
> ½ tsp each: pepper, crumbled rosemary
> 2 C chicken broth

188

4 pkgs thawed frozen artichoke hearts
1½ T lemon juice

Heat the oil, sauté onion and carrots over medium low heat, stirring until tender for 10-15 minutes. Sprinkle with flour and seasonings; stir to remove any lumps and add the broth to make a sauce (see METHODS). Stir/cook to thicken smoothly for 10 minutes. Add the artichoke hearts, cover and simmer 8-10 minutes until they are tender. Stir in the lemon juice, and transfer to the buffet table warmer.

ASPERGES CHINOIS—for 6

2 pkgs frozen asparagus tips, partially thawed
¼ C oil
2 tsp Worcestershire

Slice the asparagus on the bias, about ¼" thick. Heat oil and Worcestershire, and sauté asparagus over high heat, stirring briskly for 5-6 minutes until crisp-tender.
NOTE: You can use frozen broccoli this same way.

SWEET-SOUR BRUSSELS SPROUTS—for 6-8

3 pkgs frozen Brussels sprouts
3 T butter
1 peeled yellow onion, minced
¼ C flour
2 C beef broth
⅛ tsp ground cloves
1 tsp salt
½ tsp pepper
2 T each: brown sugar, lemon juice

Cook the sprouts in water for 5-7 minutes until crisp-tender. Sauté the onion in butter over low heat until gilded. Add the flour to onion pan and stir lightly to brown. Add beef broth for a sauce (see METHODS), and stir 10-12 minutes until smoothly thickened. Add everything else, ending with the drained sprouts. Cover and simmer over lowest heat for 5 minutes.

CARROTES CURAÇAO—for 6-8

> 2 pkgs carrots, scraped and thin-sliced
> 6 T melted butter
> 1 T sugar
> ½ tsp each: nutmeg, salt, pepper
> 2 T Curaçao

Cook the carrots *very* tender in water to cover for about 20-25 minutes. Drain, reserving a bit of cooking liquor. Mash the carrots thoroughly; add butter and seasonings. If the texture seems too dry, moisten with a bit of the cooking water—I never seem to need it. Add the Curaçao just before serving, stirring to mix well. You can use Grand Marnier instead of Curaçao.

BAKED SHREDDED CARROTS—for 4, or double-triple for a buffet

> 1 pkg carrots, scraped and coarse-shredded on the grater
> Juice and ½ grated rind of an orange
> ½ C melted butter
> 1 tsp salt
> ½ tsp pepper

Shred the carrots into an ungreased casserole, with orange rind and juice. Cover and bake 30 minutes at 325. At serving time, season and add the melted butter, stirring to mix well.

FEZ CARROTS—for 6-8

2 pkgs carrots, scraped and thin-sliced
6 T butter
½ peeled white onion, shaved thin
¼ C dry white wine
½ tsp nutmeg
½ C seedless raisins
2 T dark brown sugar

Melt butter in a large skillet, add everything but raisins and sugar. Cover and cook over lowest possible heat for nearly an hour, shaking the pan occasionally. Plump the raisins in a little warm water for about 10 minutes. When carrots are tender, add drained raisins and sugar. Stir and shake the pan 3-4 minutes to warm through.

DEVILED CARROTS—for 4

1 pkg carrots, scraped and cut lengthwise in matchsticks
½ C butter
2 T light brown sugar
¾ tsp salt
1 tsp dry mustard
⅛ tsp pepper
2 dashes cayenne

Sauté carrots in melted butter over medium heat for 5-6 minutes. Add everything else, stirring to blend well. Cover and cook over medium heat 10-12 minutes until tender, shaking the pan occasionally.

CHAYOTE

This is one of the ones that, if you never met it before, how long does it take to cook? If there are any Puerto Ricans in your vicinity, chayote will emerge in the supermarket vegetables. It is ice-green in color, and bumpy of skin with seeds inside—and it tastes a bit the way isinglass looks: crisp. I don't say it will become a family favorite, but it's fun to try.

One pound of chayotes makes 4 servings. Pare, slice, discard seeds, and cook in boiling salted water 10-15 minutes until tender. Drain, and serve with plain melted butter . . . or you can be fancy:

CHAYOTES RELLENOS—for 6

6 small whole chayotes
4 tsp flour
¼ C butter
½ lb mushrooms, coarse-cut
1 T minced chives
½ C milk
1 tsp salt
¼ tsp pepper
⅛ tsp mace
2 hardboiled eggs, coarse-cut
2 tsp lemon juice
buttered crumbs for topping

Cook the whole chayotes 5-6 minutes in boiling salted water to cover until they are crisp-tender. Drain; cool until you can handle them. Halve and remove seeds. Carefully scoop out some of the pulp, leaving a chayote shell. Coarsely mash the pulp.

Brown the flour in a small skillet, stirring over medium high heat until it becomes a handsome beige tint—set aside.

Sauté mushrooms and chives in melted butter until tender, stirring over medium heat for about 10 minutes. Scoop out the mushrooms, add the browned flour to pan fat and stir to blend well. Slowly thin with the milk for a sauce (see METHODS), and cook over low heat until smoothly thickened, adding seasonings. When the sauce is finished, add mushrooms, chayote pulp and coarse-cut eggs. Heat through over lowest flame, mixing gently.

Apportion among the chayote shells, sprinkle with buttered crumbs, and bake uncovered 10-15 minutes at 375 until lightly browned. Serve with wedges of fresh lemon to squeeze atop.

HARICOTS EN CASSEROLE—for 6

2 pkgs French-cut frozen beans, thawed
½ C diced celery
½ lb quartered mushrooms
1 peeled white onion, grated
3 pimientos, diced
½ C grated sharp Cheddar
4 T each: butter, flour
2 C hot chicken broth
½ tsp each: dry mustard, salt, pepper
1 tsp Worcestershire
¼ tsp thyme
½ C seasoned stuffing crumbs (for topping)

Make a sauce of butter, flour, broth and seasonings (see METHODS). When smoothly thickened, add everything else but crumbs. Set in a large greased casserole, top with the crumbs, and bake uncovered 30 minutes at 350.

HARICOTS VERTS PROVENÇALE—for 6

    2 pkgs frozen French-style green beans
    3 T olive oil
    1 clove peeled pressed garlic
    2 minced anchovy fillets
    1 T each: minced parsley, minced scallions, white vin-
        egar

Cook the beans in a steamer basket for 7-8 minutes over briskly simmering water until crisp-tender. Remove from heat.

Heat oil with garlic, add everything else but vinegar and beans. Stir/cook over low heat 5 minutes until scallions are tender. Add the beans, and stir for 3 minutes in the pan. Scoop out to a warmed dish, swill out the pan with the vinegar, pour over the beans and serve.

LEEKS IN ARMAGNAC—for 6-8 (or hors d'oeuvre for 12)

    12 leeks
    3 T olive oil
    1 T salt
    ¼ tsp thyme
    ⅓ C chicken broth
    ¼ C Armagnac
    Juice of ½ lemon
    1 T minced fresh parsley

This is a recipe to serve hot for dinner, or cold for an hors d'oeuvre plate; if the latter, cut the leeks in half crossways when you've finished cleaning them. At today's prices they go further as hors d'oeuvre! Leeks are apt to be very silty in the upper leaves; cut in half lengthwise and soak in cold water. Drain well, and brown in the olive oil over medium high heat for 7-10 minutes, turning gently from side to side. Add everything else. Stir/cook briskly for 10 minutes over medium high heat. Reduce to an absolute simmer, cover and cook until just-tender, about 15-20 minutes. Add the lemon juice and taste for seasoning; you may want a bit more salt or pepper. Heat through for 1 minute, and serve sprinkled with parsley.

If you mean to use as hors d'oeuvre, transfer to a shallow refrigerator dish. Dress with a mixture of 1 T lemon juice mixed with 3 T olive oil. Cover and chill thoroughly.

FRENCH MUSHROOMS—for 4

        1 lb sliced fresh mushrooms
        ½ C butter
        1½ T flour
        ½ C dry white wine
        ½ tsp each: salt, pepper
        1⅓ C light cream

Sauté mushrooms in butter for 5 minutes, and drain into the top of a double boiler. Set aside the mushrooms temporarily.

Make a sauce (see METHODS) out of 2 T mushroom pan fat, flour, and everything else, stir/cooking over boiling water for 10 minutes until smoothly thickened. Return the mushrooms, heat through and serve.

BROILED ONION—for 4-6

2 large Spanish or Bermuda onions
⅓ C melted butter
1 tsp each: salt, pepper, oregano

Peel and slice the onions ½" thick. Set on a well-greased flat broiling pan, paint generously with melted butter, sprinkle with seasonings, and broil on one side only for 5-6 minutes until browned and tender.

SCOTCH ONIONS—for 4-6

4-6 large yellow onions, peeled
2 T each: olive oil, butter
½ tsp pepper
¼ C each: beef broth, Scotch whiskey
2 T raisins

Slice the onions 1" thick—you need two slices for each portion, but if the onions are only medium-sized, you may need an extra.

Heat butter/oil, add onion slices and sear for 2 minutes over high heat, turning once. Reduce heat sharply and add pepper and broth. Cover and simmer 10 minutes to crisp-tender. Separately, soak raisins in whiskey; when onion slices are fork tender, add the Scotch drained from raisins. Raise pan heat a bit and reduce the sauce by a third. Finally add raisins, heat through without boiling for about 3 minutes, and serve.

CASSEROLE DE POIS CHINOIS—for 14-16

1 lb sliced mushrooms
¼ C butter
4 pkgs thawed frozen peas (*petits pois* are best)
1 can drained bean sprouts (1 lb size)
1 can drained sliced water chestnuts (10 oz)
1 can drained sliced bamboo shoots (6 oz)
2 cans condensed mushroom soup
½ can of milk to thin the soup
2 cans French-fried onions
½ C toasted blanched almond slivers

In general, I deplore the tinned soup sauces, but this works rather well for a large buffet casserole.

Sauté mushrooms in butter for 5-7 minutes over medium low heat. Combine with peas, Chinese vegetables, almonds and soup. Mix gently; if it seems too heavy in texture, thin slightly with a bit more milk—use your judgment, remembering it will coagulate even more during baking.

Set in a large casserole. Top with the French-fried onions, coarsely crumbled, and bake 20-25 minutes at 350. You can use a large tin of Chinese noodles instead of the onions, if you like.

BAKED PLANTAINS—for 4

4 VERY brown-skinned plantains—extremely ripe!

Wrap unpeeled in aluminum foil and bake 30-40 minutes at 350. Serve in the foil, as for baked potatoes—or open in the kitchen, skin the plantains and mash with lashings of butter.

SPINACH MADEIRA—for 6

    2 lb fresh spinach
    ¼ C water
    4 T butter
    ⅛ tsp nutmeg
    ½ tsp each: salt, pepper
    ¼ C heavy cream
    ¼ lb sliced mushrooms
    2 T Madeira
    1 C trimmed white bread cubes—½"

Blanch the spinach in water for 10 minutes covered over medium high heat; drain and chop finely. Drain again very thoroughly! Combine with 1 T butter, seasonings and cream. Separately, sauté the mushrooms in 1 T butter over medium heat for 4-5 minutes. Add to the spinach with the wine, and stir gently to blend well.

Sauté the bread cubes in remaining 2 T butter, shaking the pan briskly over medium high heat until the cubes are lightly browned and crisp (add more butter if needed). Serve these croutons on top of the spinach.

BUFFET SPINACH—for 8-10

    4 lb fresh spinach
    1 C boiling water
    ¼ C melted butter
    ½ tsp each: salt, pepper
    2 C crisp plain croutons
    Mornay Sauce (good old "see METHODS" again)

Blanch the spinach in boiling water for 10 minutes over high heat until wilted. Drain and chop finely. Drain again—and again—and again! Stir in the salt and pepper.

Make a layer 1½–2″ deep in a greased baking dish and set aside.

The Sauce:

> 2 T butter
> 3 T flour
> 2 dashes cayenne
> ¼ tsp dry mustard
> ½ tsp Dijon wet mustard
> 1 scant cup of milk
> ¼ C grated Parmesan
> 3 T light cream

Make the sauce as usual, cooking the butter/flour 2-3 minutes, adding seasonings and slowly thinning with milk. Stir over low heat 10-12 minutes until smoothly thickened, add cheese and cream. Simmer 2-3 minutes, stirring to blend well. Pour this evenly over the spinach, covering completely. Distribute the croutons on top, sprinkle with more grated Parmesan (¼ C) and dribble ¼ C melted butter over the whole thing. Set under the broiler for 4-5 minutes until the top is lightly browned.

DILLED YELLOW SQUASH—for 2

> ½ peeled yellow onion, coarse-grated
> 2 T butter
> 2 unpeeled yellow summer squash, sliced
> ½ tsp each: dill weed, salt, pepper
> ⅛ tsp garlic powder
> ¼ C bouillon

Sauté onion in butter until soft, stirring over low heat for

5-7 minutes. Add everything else, and stir/cook over low heat for 4-5 minutes more.

ZUCCHINI PATTIES—for 4

Unpeeled zucchini—1 large or 2 small
1 peeled white onion
1 egg
¼ tsp tarragon
½ tsp each: salt, pepper
2-3 T flour
2 T butter
1 T olive oil

This one requires commonsense. What you are going to DO is to grate the zucchini coarsely, as well as the onion . . . and depending on how much you have, you may need to adjust other ingredients. The egg should be lightly beaten. Combine with squash, onion and seasonings. Add the flour last, by tablespoons, stirring to mix well. You may need only a few tablespoons—or considerably more in order to hold the mixture together. However, it should not be too heavy.

Cook in mixed butter/oil by modest tablespoons; do not make the patties too big. Use medium-low heat, turning once or twice to brown both sides. You may need more butter/oil. The cooking will take 25-30 minutes, to be sure the patties are completely done. Drain on paper towels, and serve with a lump of butter atop.

ACORN SQUASH—for 6

3 acorn squash—large enough to serve ½ per person
1 C fresh bread crumbs
¼ C butter

½ C grated Parmesan
3 T dark-brown sugar

Bake the squash whole for 45-50 minutes at 350, or until fork tender. Cut in half, discard seeds. Sauté bread crumbs in butter over medium heat until lightly browned and crisp. Combine sugar and cheese; distribute among the squash halves, top with the crumbs and return to the hot oven for 3-4 minutes to heat through.

GREEN TOMATOES FROM THE GARDEN—for 6

6 large grass-green tomatoes, unpeeled
¼ C dark-brown sugar
2 tsp each: salt, pepper
¼ C each: water, dry white wine
1 C sour cream

Clip off the stem ends of the washed tomatoes and cut in half. Set in a baking dish. Apportion sugar, salt and pepper over the tomatoes; pour water and wine around the base. Cover with foil and bake 30 minutes at 350. Carefully remove to the dinner plates and keep warm. Stir sour cream into pan juices, heat 1 minute without boiling, and pour over tomatoes to serve.

CURRIED TOMATOES—for 6

6 ripe peeled tomatoes
1 C tomato sauce
2 tsp curry
2 T tart currant or grape jelly
¼ C grated sharp Cheddar
Dry bread crumbs

Set the whole tomatoes in a buttered baking dish. Combine tomato sauce, curry and jelly over low heat, and stir without boiling for 5 minutes. Pour over the tomatoes. Sprinkle with cheese and crumbs. Bake 15 minutes at 425, and serve very hot.

NOTE: This is good for Sunday brunch—accompanied by six fluffy little omelets.

HETE BLIKSEM—for 6-8

    12 large tart cooking apples
    1 T cinnamon
    3 medium-sized celeriac
    ½ to ¾ C chicken broth
    2 lb Idaho potatoes
    ¼ C butter
    1 tsp each: salt, pepper
    2 T lemon juice

Peel, core and slice the apples; set in a large pot over low heat with a little water (¼ C). Cover and create applesauce, stirring occasionally to prevent sticking. Use a wooden spoon and mash the apples ruthlessly whenever you stir. When well cooked down (about 20 minutes), put through the purée mill and stir in the cinnamon. Do NOT add any sugar.

Peel the celeriac, cut in hunks and boil tender in salted water for 15-20 minutes. Drain and set in the blender with a little of the chicken broth—you may not need it all, depending on how big the hunks of celeriac are. Turn it into a *thick* lumpy purée; it doesn't have to be velvet smooth.

Peel the potatoes, boil in salted water until tender. Turn them into fluffy mashed potatoes, using all the butter, salt and pepper. Add more butter, if you feel like it.

Finally fold celeriac into potatoes with lemon juice . . .

then swirl the applesauce into the potato mixture, stirring as if for a Marble Cake. Don't blend completely, you want streaks of applesauce running through the potato. Set in a buttered 2-quart soufflé dish or casserole, making fancy peaks and twiddles on top with your spoon. Bake 30 minutes at 400. Transfer to the broiler for 2 minutes to gild the top just before serving.

Vegetable combination dishes are innumerable and every country in the world has a version of French Ratatouille, which is the granddaddy. You'll find a recipe in any book, including *Simple Gourmet Cookery*—but actually nobody needs directions. What it *IS* is fresh vegetables—from the garden, if you're lucky enough to have one—set in layers in a deep Dutch oven with as much garlic as you like and olive oil dribbled over, plus judicious seasoning of salt, pepper, rosemary, thyme, or what-you-will. You then cover and either cook it down over low heat, or bake covered in the oven, until everything is tender. Allow 20-30 minutes for stove top, 30-45 minutes in a 300 oven, and do not stir the pot!

Any of these combinations can be served hot, or chilled as part of antipasto or hors d'oeuvres, or as a buffet accompaniment. Once you get the hang of it, it's one of the simplest possible inventions to cover all seasons!

ALBANIAN RATATOUILLE—for 8-10 at a buffet table

   10 potatoes, peeled and thin-sliced (NOT Idaho
       potatoes)
   6 ripe peeled tomatoes, coarse-cut

6 scraped carrots, thin-sliced
½ C coarse-cut celery
5 peeled yellow onions, thin-sliced
4 peeled garlic cloves, pressed
⅓ C minced fresh parsley
2 tsp each: salt, pepper
3 C water
½ C olive oil (reserve till I tell you)

Set the peeled thin slices of potato on the bottom of a large shallow greased baking dish. Mix everything else together lightly in a big bowl, and distribute over the top of the potatoes. Pour the water around the base of the dish, and bake uncovered 45 minutes at 375. *Now* you dribble the olive oil over the top, and bake another 15-20 minutes. Serve hot or cold.

CHINESE RATATOUILLE—for 8-10

1 medium head of Chinese cabbage, cut in 1" slices
4 scraped carrots, thin-sliced
2 pkgs frozen baby lima beans, thawed
1 pkg frozen snowpeas, thawed
1 large peeled seeded cucumber, coarse-sliced
½ lb whole fresh mushrooms (cut in half if large)
1 drained tin of bamboo shoots, sliced
½ C oil
1 T soy sauce
2 C chicken broth
2 T sherry
2 tsp sugar
1 tsp each: salt, pepper
4 T cornstarch dissolved in ½ C water

Heat ½ C oil in a large skillet—use a wok, if you have one—and sauté the vegetables, stirring over fairly high heat. Do the cabbage first (4 minutes). Add carrots (2 minutes), lima beans (2 minutes). Add snowpeas, cucumber, mushrooms, bamboo shoots (cook 2 minutes). Add everything else but cornstarch. Reduce heat to absolute simmer. Cover and cook 5 minutes. Add cornstarch, and stir 5-6 minutes until smoothly thickened. Serve hot or chilled.

I do not always serve a starch, particularly for the sitdown dinner party. Something depends on the age of the guests: the older they are, the more calorie-conscious! Buffet entrées often require rice for mopping up the sauce, but even so, people rarely take a large portion, which means 1 C of raw rice will probably serve six instead of the customary four.

PIGNON PILAU—for 4-6

> 1 C raw rice
> 3 T butter
> ¼ C unsalted pistachio nuts
> ½ C pine nuts
> 1 tsp mace

Cook the rice in your usual way, and keep warm. Melt the butter and sauté all the nuts over medium low heat, stirring constantly for 3-4 minutes until pine nuts are light gold. Add the rice and the mace; stir to blend thoroughly, and serve.

NOTE: This is a basic recipe to double or triple for the large party . . . but go slow on the mace! It is a very *positive* flavor; add only ½ tsp for each extra cup of rice.

PERSIAN RICE—for 4-6—another basic recipe to increase as desired

    1 C raw rice
    1 C water
    2 T butter
    1 tsp salt
    1 peeled large white onion
    4 whole cloves

Stick the cloves into the sides of the onion; set it in the middle of a buttered casserole with the well-washed rice around it. Combine water, butter and salt; bring to a full boil and pour over the rice. Cover the casserole *tightly*, and bake 30 minutes at 325. Uncover, lower heat to 250, and dry out for 5 minutes.

PILAF TEHERAN—for 10-12

    5 C warm chicken broth
    2½ C washed raw rice
    1 C chopped peeled yellow onions
    2 C each: chopped fresh mushrooms, golden raisins
    1 C each: blanched almonds; chopped pitted dates
    1 tsp each: salt, oregano
    ½ tsp white pepper
    6 T butter

You can use soup packets to make the broth, in which case use 8 for 5½ C water, and stir to dissolve thoroughly over low heat—bring slowly up to a boil, and you will end with the 5 C needed. For a major effect, I make my own stock; I usually have an accumulation of frozen backs, necks, giblets to simmer slowly with onion, carrot, salt and pepper in 6-7 C water. One hour should do it, and you can strip off any bits of meat to add to the pilaf—waste not, want not, but discard the giblets in the direction of your cat, who will consider it a tender attention.

Either way, you start with exactly 5 C of warm chicken broth . . . no more. Add to the rice in a big covered casserole. Bake 45 minutes at 350 until liquid is entirely absorbed. While that is doing, melt 3 T butter in a skillet and sauté onions with mushrooms until tender without browning—over low heat, stirring occasionally for 7-8 minutes.

When the rice is finished, add contents of the sauté pan plus everything else but the last 3 T of butter. If you've got some chicken shreds, they go in here, too. Mix gently but thoroughly to distribute everything through the rice. Set uncovered in the oven with the heat off for 2-3 minutes to warm through—or if the oven is on to cook something else, cover the casserole and remove after 2 minutes. Cut the rest of the butter in dots over the top of the rice and serve at once.

Rice is not the only accompaniment for mopping up, and sometimes it is fun to startle your guests with an unfamiliar dish.

CERNY KUBA—for 4, but easily expanded to any number

½ C pearl barley
1½ C water
½ tsp each: salt, caraway seed
½ C sliced mushrooms

3 T butter
1 T minced fresh parsley
1 peeled garlic clove, pressed
¼ tsp marjoram
⅛ tsp pepper
¼ C additional butter

Simmer the barley in water with salt and caraway seed for 1 hour over very low heat, or until the barley is very tender. Do NOT drain!

Separately sauté the mushrooms in 3 T butter, stirring occasionally over medium low heat for 10 minutes until tender.

Combine all remaining ingredients, and mash together into a smooth paste.

Put everything into a casserole, stirring to mix well. Cover and bake 30 minutes at 325. This goes nicely with roast pork or fresh ham.

TARHONYA—for 6

½ C peeled chopped yellow onions
1½ C egg barley
¼ C butter
½ tsp pepper
1 tsp salt
3 C beef or chicken stock

Melt the butter and sauté onions over medium low heat until soft without browning. Add the barley, and stir for 3-4 minutes to gild lightly. Add everything else, cover and simmer 25-30 minutes over lowest possible heat, checking occasionally. Add a bit of water or extra stock if needed to prevent sticking.

This can also be baked in a covered casserole for 30-40

minutes at 300, checking occasionally. This is a Hungarian dish to serve instead of potatoes.

PULISKA—for 6

    3 C water
    2 tsp salt
    1 C yellow cornmeal
    1½ C lekvar (plum jam)
    1½ C sour cream

Bring water and salt to a brisk boil, transfer to the top of a double boiler over boiling water, and slowly pour in the cornmeal. Stir constantly! Reduce heat to hold the water in the bottom pot at a low simmer-boil, cover the cornmeal and cook 20 minutes. Stir occasionally, and add boiling water to the lower pot if needed—it's apt to boil away. You should end with a thick cornmeal mush.

Spread half the mush on the bottom of a buttered casserole, spread the lekvar evenly on top, and cover with remaining cornmeal. Finally, spread over the sour cream and bake uncovered for 10 minutes at 375. This is a good luncheon dish in cold weather, or instead of potatoes to accompany roast pork or ham.

NOTE: Lekvar is a *very* stiff European jam; New Yorkers can get it from Lekvar by the Barrel, 1577 First Avenue (82nd Street). Almost none of the ordinary commercial jams can substitute, with the possible exception of guava jelly. Nothing is sufficiently stiff, and will result in a gooey mess. However, you can substitute grated sharp Cheddar . . . or you can make your own stiff purée out of stewed dried apricots.

Baked beans are traditional for the smorgasbord table, with a pot of warmed cocktail frankfurters on one side and a pot of Swedish meatballs with sour cream on the other.

BUFFET BEANS—for 18-20

    6 *large* tins of baked beans WITHOUT tomato sauce
    6 large yellow onions, peeled and thin-sliced
    1 C each: molasses, dark brown sugar
    ¼ C Worcestershire
    1 T baking soda, dissolved in 2 T warm water
    ½ C soluble coffee crystals
    2 C Bourbon
    ½ C dry mustard
    Hot water as required

Add dissolved soda to the molasses, stirring to mix.

Set the beans in a large bowl, and add everything but coffee and Bourbon. Stir gently, but mix well. Sprinkle the soluble coffee evenly over the top and add the whiskey. Gently turn and mix to incorporate everything. Cover and store overnight at room temperature.

To cook: stir/mix the beans thoroughly and transfer to a suitable baking pan or deep casserole. Bake 30 minutes at 400.

NOTE: You *can* add Vienna sausage or cocktail franks directly to the pan, if you like—or decorate the top with tinned pineapple rings and maraschino cherries.

BARBECUE BEANS—for 8-10

    2 C dried lima beans
    2 peeled garlic cloves
    2 tsp salt
    6 T butter

3 C grated sharp Cheddar
½ C Sauterne

Soak the beans overnight in water to cover; drain and set aside until an hour before serving. Then cover with fresh cold water, add garlic cloves, cover the pot, bring to a boil and sharply reduce heat to simmer 40 minutes. Add the salt, raise heat to high and boil uncovered for 15 minutes to reduce the liquid. Again, sharply reduce the heat and add everything else. Simmer uncovered over very low heat until cheese melts. Do NOT stir too vigorously, or the end product will be mushy! This goes for a patio party of B-q'd ribs with lots of green salad.

BHOONEE KICHREE—for 6-8

1 C each: raw rice, uncooked lentils
2 peeled yellow onions, sliced
¼ C butter
2 bay leaves
1 cinnamon stick
½ tsp salt
4 each: whole peppercorns, whole cloves
3 slices of green ginger
Hot water

Melt the butter and sauté onions over low heat for 5-6 minutes until they are golden-limp but not browned; remove onions to a warm plate.

Add rice and lentils to the pan fat, and stir to coat well. Add everything else but the onions, plus just enough hot water to barely cover rice/lentils. Cover the pan and simmer over very lowest heat 16-18 minutes, shaking the pan occasionally, until all liquid is absorbed. Check around 15 minutes and add 1-2 T hot water if needed to prevent sticking. When rice is fluffy-tender, discard bay leaves, cinnamon stick, cloves and peppercorns (if you can fish them out), and serve with the sautéed onions on the top.

Potatoes for a buffet are mostly salads, or scalloped, and anybody knows how to do them, although curry is a nice change.

KARIN'S CURRIED POTATOES—for 8-10

10-12 potatoes
½ C mushrooms, minced
⅓ C peeled yellow onion, minced
1½-2 C milk
⅓ C sharp Cheddar
¼ C Swiss cheese
2 T butter
1 T each: chives, curry powder
¼ tsp turmeric
½ tsp each: basil, white pepper
1 tsp salt
½ tsp celery seed
¾ tsp tarragon
Paprika and parsley flakes for topping

Parboil potatoes *firm*-tender; peel and thin-slice. Combine milk, cheeses, butter, all spices and herbs in a saucepan. Simmer over very low heat, stirring often to blend well for a smoothly melted sauce—about 15 minutes. Remove from heat and add minced onions and mushrooms.

Set a layer of potatoes in the bottom of a casserole, cover

with some of the sauce, and repeat the layers until all is used, ending with the sauce. Sprinkle with paprika and parsley for color, and bake 20-25 minutes at 350 until nicely browned and bubbling.

CATALAN—for 8

4 large peeled Idaho potatoes, thin-sliced
4 large peeled yellow onions, thin-sliced
¼ C olive oil
1 pimiento, diced
¼ tsp saffron, soaked in 1 T warm water
½ tsp salt
¼ C coarse-chopped blanched almonds

Sauté potatoes, onions and pimiento in olive oil over medium heat, turning gently to brown the potato slices while keeping onions transparent. When the potatoes start to color (10 minutes), add salt and saffron in its soak water. Cover the pan, reduce heat to absolute minimum and cook 15 minutes, shaking the pan or stirring to prevent sticking. Add the almonds, cook 5 more minutes and serve.

NOTE: This can be done successfully in an electric frying pan, and transferred to the buffet table to finish cooking with thermostat turned to Warm. Also, it doubles easily for more guests.

GRATIN DAUPHINOIS—for 6

1 lb potatoes, peeled and thin-sliced (NOT Idahos)
1 peeled garlic clove
1 C heavy cream
¼ C butter
Salt, pepper, nutmeg

For this, you need what is known as "old" potatoes—the big dusty ones that are not Idahos, because those would cook into mashed potato. Soak the sliced potatoes in cold water to cover for 20 minutes; drain and pat dry on towelling.

Prepare a casserole: cut the garlic clove in half and rub the casserole thoroughly. Next smear some of the butter inside the casserole. Finally, make layers of the potato slices. Press all the garlic, and insert it judiciously between the layers —EACH of which you sprinkle with 2 dashes of salt, 2 dashes of nutmeg, and 2 hearty twists of the pepper mill.

When the potatoes are all in place, pour over the cream and cut the butter in bits across the top. Cover and bake 1 hour at 300. Uncover and bake 20 minutes. Raise the heat to 400 for 10 minutes, to set a golden crust on the top of the potatoes.

Salads

These are the major back-up for any buffet, smorgasbord, patio party or church social—and equally indispensable for a lunch or dinner party at table. Salads start with the dressing—which may be plain or fancy, but are always basically of two kinds: thick, or thin. *Thick* is mayonnaise and the boiled dressings that are a version of white sauce . . . and *thin* is the Vinaigrette combination of oil with vinegar or lemon juice. True French or Vinaigrette dressing is 1 measure of vinegar (or lemon juice) to 3 of good-quality olive oil, plus seasonings to your taste. I have never yet been able to buy this in a bottle, but why bother, when it is so simple to make your own?

Once you have mastered that basic 1 to 3 proportion, you can use *any* measure: it can be kitchen tablespoons, the salad mixing spoon, or 1 cup to 3 cups. What's needed is a guage of how much to make, although Vinaigrette will last indefinitely in a tight-capped refrigerator bottle. Just remember to let the jar reach room temperature and shake it up like mad before pouring over tonight's effort. I prefer to make it fresh, principally because I can never remember which vinegar and herbs I used for the leftover in the fridge.

215

For prepared salads on individual plates—that is, lettuce with SOMETHING on top—½ C of Vinaigrette will suffice for 4-6 portions. If you are using a thick-style dressing, 2 T is enough per serving. I am speaking here of the salads served to accompany lunch or dinner plates.

For the tossed salad, the proportions of oil, vinegar and seasonings can be added more light-heartedly. It will not matter if measurements are not exact. By the time it is adequately tossed and transferred to salad bowls, any excess will drain into the bottom of the mixing bowl. What is wanted for the mixed greens is only a light coating. You do not wish a plate swimming in Vinaigrette or masked by a thick dressing.

CUCUMBER DRESSING—for mixed greens

    1 cucumber, peeled and seeded
    1 C mayonnaise

Purée the cucumber in the blender and combine with the mayonnaise, adding a bit of coarse-ground black pepper if you like. Set the salad in individual bowls, add a sliced red radish or tomato wedge for color, and apportion the dressing on top—serves 6-8.

MAYONNAISE DIJON—asparagus tips for 6-8

    2 boxes frozen asparagus tips
    2 T Dijon mustard
    1 tsp Worcestershire
    ⅛ tsp curry powder
    2 T heavy cream
    2 tsp lemon juice

Steam the asparagus crisp-tender, and chill thoroughly. Combine everything else, mixing smooth; cover and chill. Serves 6-8, at lunch.

CHUTNEY DRESSING—for 8-10

1 C each: mayonnaise, chili sauce
½ C heavy cream
¼ C drained chopped chutney
2 tsp peeled grated white onion

Mix smoothly together, and use on prepared salad bowls of mixed greens, halved cherry tomatoes, sliced radishes and quartered hardboiled eggs.

CITY CLUB DRESSING—for 4-6

⅔ C sugar
1 tsp each: dry mustard, paprika
¼ tsp salt
⅓ C each: honey, white vinegar
1 C olive oil
1 T onion juice
1-2 T lemon juice
1½ tsp celery seed

Combine sugar, seasonings, honey and vinegar; cook/ stir over low heat until sugar melts—about 5 minutes, and do not allow it to boil! Transfer to the blender with oil and onion juice. Buzz smooth, adding 1 T lemon juice first; if needed, add the second. The final consistency should be quite thick and translucent. Stir in the celery seed last. Chill very slightly, and use for a fresh fruit luncheon salad.

CAVIAR MAYONNAISE—for 4-6 dinner guests

½ C mayonnaise
¼ C sour cream
1 oz black caviar
4 tsp ketchup
¼ tsp onion juice
1 tsp lemon juice
⅛ tsp pepper

Combine everything but caviar, stirring very smooth; cover and chill 1 hour. Add the caviar just before serving, stirring to mix gently. Use on endive or firm small wedges of iceberg lettuce.

AVOCADO DRESSING—#1 for hearts of palm at dinner

1 peeled ripe avocado
4 tsp lemon juice
½ tsp salt
1 C sour cream
1 tsp grated white onion
¼ C milk
4 drops hot pepper seasoning
½ tsp dill weed

Set everything in the blender and buzz very smooth. Cover and chill thoroughly. Serve on drained hearts of palm on watercress.

NOTE: Hearts of palm are a bit uncertain: you never know how many will be in the tin! Figure two small hearts, one very large halved lengthways, per person. Buy two tins for four people, but you may be able to stretch for six. This amount of dressing will be enough.

AVOCADO DRESSING—#2 for sliced oranges or mixed fresh fruit

   1 peeled ripe avocado, cut in hunks
   1 C creamed cottage cheese
   1 tsp sugar
   1 T mayonnaise
   ¼ tsp salt
   3 T lemon juice
   ¼ C orange juice

   Set all in the blender and buzz smooth—enough for 4 at lunch.

AVOCADO DRESSING #3—for plain iceberg lettuce wedges at dinner

   1 peeled ripe avocado
   2 ripe tomatoes, peeled, seeded and chopped
   2 tsp grated white onion
   2 T anchovy paste
   ¼ C vinegar
   ½ C olive oil
   ½ tsp pepper

   Mash the avocado coarsely, so it has small lumps. Work onion, anchovy paste and pepper with the vinegar to smooth slightly. Combine everything, mix well, cover and chill 1 hour.

COLESLAW DRESSING—for 4-6 at a patio party

   1 T each: butter, flour
   1 tsp each: sugar, salt, dry mustard
   ½ tsp pepper

2 beaten eggs
1 C light cream
2 T vinegar

Mash together butter, flour and seasonings (*beurre manié*). Slowly add the beaten eggs, mixing to prevent lumps. Add the cream, and mix again until very smooth. Heat the vinegar *without boiling*, and slowly add to the first mixture (see METHODS), stirring gently. Set over medium-low heat and stir about 5-7 minutes until smoothly thickened. Remove and cool to room temperature. Mix with 2 C shredded green cabbage, cover and chill slightly before serving.

**DRESSING FOR SHRIMP AND
WATERCRESS**—luncheon for 4

2 C fresh unflavored yoghurt
½ tsp salt
2 T honey
¾ tsp curry powder
4 tsp lemon juice
½ tsp grated white onion
⅛ tsp paprika

Combine all and mix very smooth. Chill and add to 1 lb cooked cleaned shrimp, mixing well. Serve on beds of watercress.

Next we come to the salads one serves as make-weight on a buffet table. That is, these are meant to accompany the major dishes by a modest one or two spoonsful and provide merely a change of pace . . . but many of these can also become part of an antipasto or hors d'oeuvre table service for luncheon or dinner. Of these, the simplest is GAR-BANZOS TOUT SIMPLE—which I listed among the Antipasto recipes in the Appetizers chapter, together with CÉLERI RÉMOULADE. However, as side dishes for the buffet, these are not to be overlooked. Both can be easily expanded for any number of guests.

GARBANZOS CHILLENOS—for 8

2 cans plain chickpeas, drained
1 peeled white onion, shaved thin
½ C olive oil
¼ C lemon juice
2 tsp salt
¼ tsp white pepper
½ tsp ground coriander
1 lb cream cheese

Combine oil, lemon juice and seasonings; pour over chickpeas and onion, coating thoroughly. Cover and chill at least 1 hour. Set the cream cheese in the freezer for 10 minutes until it is very firm. With a sharp knife, dice it into ½" cubes. Cover and return to the fridge until serving time. At the final moment, combine everything, stirring very lightly to mix. Transfer to a chilled bowl lined with shredded lettuce. This must be served icy cold!

FEODOR—for 10

6 large cucumbers
1 T salt
3 hardboiled eggs

¾ C sour cream
½ tsp vinegar
1 T fresh-ground pepper (maybe more)

If the cucumbers are supermarket, peel and seed—if they are garden-fresh (lucky you!) peel and don't seed. You'll probably need one or two extra if they are small-sized.

Dice the cucumber, sprinkle with salt and mix about. After 20 minutes, drain thoroughly, rinse briefly in cold water and drain again. Combine fine-chopped eggs with sour cream, vinegar and pepper. Mix gently with diced cucumber, and sprinkle with more black pepper or perhaps a dash of paprika? Serve in a lettuce-lined glass dish at the buffet . . . or apportion on a lettuce leaf for dinner guests.

RAW MUSHROOM SALAD—for 8-10

24 *large* fresh white mushrooms
2 T lemon juice
2 peeled garlic cloves
½ C olive oil
¼ C each: Roquefort, cream cheese
1 tsp salt
½ tsp pepper
1 T Worcestershire

Slice unpeeled mushrooms Chinese-fashion, sprinkle with lemon juice, cover and chill 1 hour. Press the garlic cloves and mash very thoroughly into the olive oil. Mash the cheese smoothly together at room temperature, working in seasonings and finally thinning with the garlic/oil to a liquid paste. Drain any excess lemon juice from the mushrooms and discard. Pour cheese dressing over mushrooms, mixing to coat well, and serve in a lettuce-lined bowl.

ACCOMPANIMENT SHRIMP—for 8

½ C each: mayonnaise, Vinaigrette
2 T each: chopped drained capers, sweet gherkins,
    parsley
1 T ketchup
2 lb cooked cleaned shrimp

Combine mayonnaise and Vinaigrette smoothly, add everything else—shrimp last. Cover and chill 1-2 hours. Serve in a lettuce-lined bowl, garnished with hardboiled egg slices and a bit of paprika.

NOTE: This is not really substantial enough for a main dish, but makes an excellent change of pace when the Big Presentation is (perhaps) a whole turkey or ham. It is a good component of the smorgasbord, where you are offering both hot and cold dishes, plus sweet and tart gelatins—and obviously it can be expanded for any number of guests.

CHICKEN FOR LUNCH—serves 4

1 C mayonnaise
1 tsp onion juice
2 dashes cayenne
¼ tsp ground cumin
½ tsp salt
2 C cooked diced chicken
½ C each: thin-sliced celery, toasted almond slivers
1-2 T milk (perhaps)

Combine mayonnaise with seasonings, mixing smooth— thin with a bit of milk, if needed; the dressing should not be too stiff. Combine with chicken, celery, almonds and coat completely. Cover and chill 1 hour.

THANKSGIVING SATURDAY BUFFET—for 12-14

4 C cooked diced chicken or turkey (what else?)
1 C each: sliced celery, coarse-cut pecans, tart peeled
    diced apple
1½ C mayonnaise
½ C sour cream
½ tsp ground cardamom
1 tsp grated lemon peel
1 small white onion, peeled and grated
2 T minced parsley
3 dashes cayenne

Combine everything from mayonnaise down the list, mixing smoothly. Taste carefully; you may want a bit of salt and pepper. The consistency should be fairly thin in order to cover all the other ingredients; if necessary, add a bit of milk.

Combine turkey, nuts, celery, apple; pour over the dressing, and mix well. Cover and chill to serving time.

CHICKEN ORIENTALE—for 10-12

3 chickens—3-4 lb each (see below)
3 C diced celery
½ C minced peeled yellow onion
2 T curry powder
½ C heavy cream
3 C mayonnaise
½ C golden raisins
1 can drained water chestnuts, thin-sliced

With respect to the chickens: you may use 2 fricasee hens, or buy 10 lb of wings and drumsticks, for the sake of economy. What's wanted is an end product of 5-6 lb cooked diced chicken meat. In all cases, cook your chicken tender in simmering water to cover. Cool, strip off the meat, combine with celery, onion, raisins and water chestnuts. Cover and chill.

Dissolve curry powder in cream, and blend with the mayonnaise. Taste critically; you may want a bit of salt and pepper. Coat the chicken mixture thoroughly, and chill until serving time. Decorate the bowl with sprigs of watercress or parsley.

JELLIED GUACAMOLE—buffet for 8-10

    4 large ripe peeled mashed avocados
    2 small ripe tomatoes, peeled, seeded and fine-chopped
    1 peeled white onion, fine-minced
    2 T each: mayonnaise, lemon juice
    1 tsp salt
    2 dashes Tabasco
    2½ C chicken broth
    3 packets of gelatin (3 T unflavored)
    4 bacon slices, crisp-cooked, drained and fine-crumbled
    1 pimiento cut in small dice

Combine the first six ingredients, creating the guacamole. Soften gelatin in ½ C chicken broth, add remaining chicken broth, and dissolve over hot water. Stir into the avocado mixture. Prepare a 2-quart ring mold with crumbled bacon and pimiento bits tastefully disposed about the bottom. Gently pour in the guacamole—try not to disturb the garnish. Chill firm for 3-4 hours. Unmold on a lettuce-lined platter, and fill the center of the ring with watercress.

AVOCADO MOLD—lunch for 6-8

3 large ripe peeled mashed avocados
1 C sour cream
3 gelatin packets
½ C cold water
1 C boiling water
¼ C lemon juice
¼ tsp salt

Soften gelatin in cold water, dissolve in the boiling water. Add salt and lemon juice, and stir 10-15 minutes off heat until it becomes syrupy. Combine avocado purée with sour cream, and taste for flavor; you may want some pepper, but NO salt because it's in the gelatin. Finally combine everything, mixing thoroughly. Pour into a rinsed 8-cup mold and chill 2-3 hours until firm.

STUFFED LETTUCE—luncheon for 4-6

1 large, very tight, head of iceberg lettuce
4 oz each: Roquefort, cream cheese
1 pimiento, minced
2 T each: minced scallion, minced black olives, minced parsley
1 tsp Worcestershire
2 T mayonnaise

Hold lettuce aside while you mash everything else smoothly together. With a sharp knife, hollow out the firm center of the lettuce to form a shell—use your judgment on how much to remove! Stuff with the cheese mixture, wrap in foil and chill very firm for several hours. Shred the lettuce you took out and use as a base for the salad plates. Slice the stuffed lettuce, set atop shreds and serve with a tablespoon of bottled Green Goddess dressing dribbled over.

BUFFET VEGETABLE SALAD—for 20

4 pkgs frozen mixed vegetables
4 large potatoes—not Idahoes!
1 bunch each: radishes, scallions, celery
1 large green pepper, seeded and shaved in thin strips
4 carrots, scraped and cut in matchsticks 1½" long
6 ripe tomatoes, peeled
½ lb fresh mushrooms
½ C each: stuffed green olives, pitted ripe olives
2 heads of iceberg lettuce
¼ C minced fresh parsley
12 hardboiled eggs
2 C mayonnaise
1 large white onion, peeled and grated
1 C milk
½ C pot cheese
Salt, pepper, paprika, garlic powder—to taste

This is my Old Faithful, because you do it yesterday, which leaves you free to concentrate on Party Day. All it requires is space in the fridge to chill overnight.

Boil the potatoes in water to cover for 20 minutes until fork-tender; drain, cool, peel. Blanch the frozen mixed vegetables in a large pot of simmering water for 10 minutes until crisp-tender—they should be definitely underdone! Drain and cool. Clean radishes, scallions and celery in plenty of cold water; thin-slice all but the tiny celery hearts (save them for garnish). Scrape the carrots and cut julienne; seed the green pepper and shave it into strips that will fit on a fork. Peel the tomatoes, set in a bowl and cover. Hardboil the eggs, shell, and leave them covered in the fridge.

NOW: combine blanched mixed vegetables in a large working bowl with radishes, scallions, carrots, green pepper and the cut celery (4 large stalks are usually enough). Cover and set in the fridge to chill overnight—along with the eggs, tomatoes and potatoes in separate covered bowls.

Combine mayonnaise and milk, stirring slowly until perfectly smooth. Add onion, parsley and pot-cheese. Do NOT season as yet! The dressing should be thin, in order to pour over the vegetables tomorrow. Cover and chill overnight.

For the final assembly:

> Quarter the mushrooms
> Drain the olives, keeping them in separate bowls
> Coarse-cut 6 of the eggs
> Seed 3 of the peeled tomatoes, and cut in hunks
> Dice all the cold potatoes

Add all but green olives to the main vegetable bowl and mix gently to distribute. Vigorously stir up the bowl of dressing; add a bit more milk if needed—the consistency should be that of thin cream. Taste critically at this point: you may want a bit more salt or pepper, a dash of garlic powder or paprika. When it tastes right to you, pour over the vegetables with abandon, and mix tenderly until everything is coated. Don't mash or bruise anything; this is why you undercooked the vegetables, so each piece could be recognized.

Finally transfer to a serving bowl handsomely lined with lettuce leaves curling up the sides and over the edges. Shred more lettuce in the bottom, and decorate the bowl with the remaining peeled tomatoes cut in wedges, the remaining eggs quartered, the tiny celery heart stalks. Cast the stuffed green olives light-heartedly over the top—and there you are: a buffet salad!

SHRIMP ELSPETH—for 16-20

    4 lb cooked cleaned shrimp
    6 T tarragon vinegar
    1 tsp dried crumbled tarragon
    ½ tsp each: salt, ground ginger, grated lemon peel
    2 T minced fresh parsley
    1 T chervil

Combine the above and marinate covered overnight in the fridge, stirring whenever you think of it. At serving time, add:

    2 C sour cream
    2 C halved cherry tomatoes
    2 peeled diced ripe avocados

Mix in the cream first, to blend smoothly with the marinade. Then add tomatoes (if big, cut in quarters) and avocado. Mix gently to distribute among the shrimps without mashing the avocado. Serve at once, or cover and chill no more than 30 minutes before transfer to the buffet table.

SHELLFISH FANCY—for 16-20 (this one is a fuss)

    3 lobsters, 2-lb each
    1 lb each: cooked cleaned shrimp, lump crabmeat, fresh salmon
    6 scraped carrots
    1 frozen pkg each: baby limas, tiny peas, French-cut beans, cauliflower
    1 C each diced: celery, radishes, seeded peeled cucumber
    6 ripe tomatoes, peeled, seeded and diced
    3 hardboiled eggs

½ tsp dry mustard
1 T each: white vinegar, salt
¼ tsp white pepper
2 T olive oil
2 T gelatin, dissolved in ½ C hot water
½ C heavy cream
½ lb soft butter
4 T heavy cream, whipped
More salt and white pepper
Lettuce
Garnishes: olives, parsley, hardboiled eggs, etc.

What you are going to DO is to make a gelatin mold of all the vegetables—accompany with assorted shellfish, and make a dressing out of the salmon. The major problem is whether you have a big enough mold for the gelatin. I have two old-fashioned fish-shaped 6 cup molds that arrange handsomely on the final platter, leaving space between for the shellfish. Two large ring molds would be equally good, or you could use a long rectangular Pyrex baking dish.

First boil and clean your lobsters; cut the meat into fork-sized bits. Reserve tomalley, and coral (if any) as well as the tail shells. In fact, save some of the small legs; they're fun as part of the garnish.

Cook and clean the shrimp; pick over crab lumps to remove shell bits. Cover and chill all the shellfishies.

Poach the salmon in simmering water to just-cover, about 15 minutes until it flakes easily. Drain, skin and bone it. Grind it finely, cover and chill.

Next, cook all the frozen vegetables and thin-sliced carrots in boiling salted water for 7-8 minutes; they should be very crisp. You can cook 'em all together in the same pot. Drain and cool.

Combine remaining vegetables with the cooked; cover and chill well.

Start dissolving the gelatin. Separately mince the hard-boiled eggs, and mix with mustard, vinegar, salt and white pepper. Mash well together and slowly stir in olive oil, beating smooth. Add the dissolved gelatin; beat well. Add the plain heavy cream and beat again. Finally fold in all the chilled vegetables, set in the mold or pan, and chill firm for 4-5 hours.

For the dressing: combine ground salmon with the soft butter, working into a smooth paste; season with ½ tsp each of salt and white pepper. Whip the 4 T heavy cream, and gently fold into the salmon. Pile this into two of the lobster tail shells, cover and chill briefly while composing the final masterpiece.

Line a large platter with a few lettuce leaves; unmold upon it the vegetable gelatin. Depending on what sort of mold you used, you pile the lobster meat in the ring centers . . . or mounded between two curving molds . . . or piled on top of the large flat rectangular job? The tail shells of salmon dressing go at either end of the platter with serving ladles. The crabmeat and shrimp is disposed decoratively in separate piles around the edges. You garnish the platter with quartered hardboiled eggs, parsley sprigs, some of the little lobster legs, a handful of assorted olives and radishes.

Spread the tomalley on plain melba toast rounds as far as it will go, and put them on a separate plate (or eat them surrepshusly in the kitchen before the guests arrive). IF you had any coral, stir it into ¼ C of mayonnaise and serve in a little bowl for the crabmeat and shrimp.

In a way, this one is a lot of work and expensive into the bargain—but all you need is a big bowl of coleslaw and plenty of hot buttered rolls.

PRAHA COLESLAW—to accompany the above

>   Green cabbage—enough to make 10 C shredded
>   2 T butter
>   2 C boiling water

4 eggs
2 T vinegar
1 C sour cream
1 tsp each: salt, pepper

Melt the butter in a pot large enough to contain all the cabbage. Set the cabbage on top of the butter, pour over the *boiling* water, cover the pot tightly and let it sit over the minimum lowest heat for 15 minutes. Drain it thoroughly.

Beat the eggs well and pour over cabbage, mixing lightly but thoroughly. Add the sour cream and seasoning; continue to mix until all the cabbage is well coated. Cover and chill for several hours. Serve icy cold.

Of course what this IS is a sort of Caesar salad made with cabbage . . . and you can add crisp croutons if you like.

Desserts

The dessert always depends upon the entrée: if it was simple, a fancy dessert is in order . . . if it was hearty and extremely flavorful, the dessert should be rather plain. This is particularly true of buffet parties, where you have offered a choice of entrées and salads. A fresh fruit compote, with or without a dash of liqueur and/or a dollop of softened vanilla ice cream, is usually the best choice. For a vaguely Oriental menu, such as Pork Taiwan, you might offer:

CURRIED FRUIT—for 10

> 8 C fruit, assorted
> 2 C dark brown sugar
> 2 T curry powder
> ⅔ C melted butter

For the fruit, use whatever is fresh in market: peeled, cored, pitted, cut in hunks . . . but you want a good variety. If it's principally apples, hard pears, grapes, oranges—as in winter—use a drained single portion can of apricots and sliced peaches to gussie up. You can literally use any fruits, from melon balls to sliced mango, pitted prunes, and persimmon; the more, the better.

Drain away excess fruit juice very thoroughly, and set in a deep casserole. Combine sugar, curry and melted butter, mixing to make a crumbly topping. Spread evenly over the fruit, and bake uncovered 1 hour at 300. Serve at room temperature with a spoonful of soft vanilla ice cream—and make the portions rather small! All that's needed is a bit—to clear the taste buds before coffee.

FROSTED GRAPES—for 8-10—good for luncheon

    2 lb seedless white grapes
    ⅔ C honey
    ¼ C each: brandy, lemon juice
    2 pints sour cream

Stem the grapes, wash and drain well. Set in a deep bowl, pour over them the honey, brandy and lemon juice. Mix gently but thoroughly to coat the grapes well. Cover and set in the fridge overnight, stirring whenever you think of it. Serve direct from the refrigerator, in small dessert dishes with a spoonful of sour cream atop.

APPLE DESSERT—for 8

    6 *large* tart cooking apples (more, if they are medium size)
    6 T vanilla sugar (sprinkle sugar with a tsp of vanilla)
    ½ C butter, melted
    10 slices trimmed white bread
    ⅓ C extra butter
    ½ C brandy, dark rum or Bourbon

Peel, core and thick-slice the apples, and sauté in ⅓ C butter over medium heat until half-cooked, sprinkling with 3 T vanilla sugar. Do not let the apples disintegrate!

Lightly toast the bread slices and butter generously. Cut each slice into 3 strips. Set a third of them on the bottom of a buttered casserole, and top with half the apples. Place another third of the toast strips on the apples, setting these at right angles to the first layer. Cover with remaining apples and top with the last toast strips set parallel to the bottom ones . . . if I make myself clear?

Sprinkle with remaining vanilla sugar, pour over the melted butter and bake 15 minutes uncovered at 400.

Warm the liquor thoroughly, light it and pour flaming over the casserole at table. Again, serve smallish portions.

NORMAN BREAD PUDDING—for 6

    14 to 16 white bread slices, trimmed
    ¼ lb melted butter
    6-8 tart cooking apples
    1 T nutmeg
    6 T sugar
    2 tsp cardamom
    2 T additional butter

What you are going to DO is to line a buttered 1-quart casserole with very thin slices of buttery bread, fitting them together in such a way as to make a smooth shell that will hang together after baking, so you can unmold onto a plate. It is imperative to have *thin* bread. If you can get an unsliced loaf, trim the crusts and wrap in waxed paper; set in the freezer for 10 to 15 minutes until it is firm enough to slice ¼" thick. If you must use commercial bread, trim and flatten ruthlessly with the rolling pin.

Paint the bread generously on both sides with melted

butter, and fit into the casserole, making a small overlap at the edges and pressing them together firmly. Save enough buttered bread slices for the top.

Fill the center of the buttered bread shell with peeled cored sliced apples, in layers, sprinkling each with mixed nutmeg-sugar-cardamom. Cut the last 2 T of butter over the apples, and top with the reserved bread slices, fitting together as neatly as you can.

Bake 50 minutes at 325, covering with foil if the top browns too quicky—which it nearly always does after a half hour. Unmold on a plate and serve warmish, with a dribble of plain heavy cream.

HONEY CREAM—for 2

    1 egg yolk
    ¼ C honey
    1 egg white, stiff-beaten
    2 T heavy cream, whipped stiff
    grated lemon peel

Beat egg yolk with honey, set in a double boiler over simmering water and stir constantly until thickened (15-20 minutes). Cool to room temperature. Mix with the egg white, fold in the whipped cream, set in two dessert dishes and chill. Serve cold with a garnish of grated lemon peel.

HONEY MOUSSE—for 2

    2 egg yolks
    ¼ C honey
    ⅔ C heavy cream, whipped
    2 T grated bitter chocolate

Beat the egg yolks lightly, combine with honey in a

double boiler over simmering water and cook/stir 15-20 minutes until thickened. Set the pan in a bowl of ice and stir until completely cooled. Add the whipped cream, pour into a small mold and freeze 3-4 hours. Decorate the servings with the chocolate.

LIQUEUR SOUFFLÉ—for 2

½ C milk
2 T sugar
1 dash of salt
2 T flour
2 egg yolks
3 egg whites
2 tsp butter
2 oz of any liqueur you like

Combine sugar, salt and flour in a saucepan; slowly add the milk, working out any lumps in the flour, and stir/cook 2-3 minutes over medium low heat until smooth. Remove from the heat, add the butter and stir to let it melt. Add the egg yolks one at a time, unbeaten, and stir vigorously to mix well. Stiff-beat the egg whites, and just before adding them, stir the liquor into egg yolk mixture. Lastly fold in the egg whites, pour into a buttered soufflé dish dusted with sugar, and bake about 40 minutes at 350.

For the liqueur, anything is good: Grand Marnier, Crème de Cassis, Cherry Heering, Crème de Cacao, Curaçao . . . but I am not mad-keen about Pernod.

ZABAGLIONE PEARS—for 6

6 pears, peeled, cored and halved
½ C sugar
2 C water

¼ C lemon juice
1 T grated rind of orange, and of lemon
⅛ tsp salt
2 cinnamon sticks

Dip the pears into lemon juice. Combine everything else and bring to a boil. Add the pears, cover and reduce to a simmer for 25-30 minutes until tender. Cool in the syrup.

For the sauce:

5 egg yolks beaten light
1 dash of salt
½ C confectioners' sugar
½ C cream sherry
½ tsp lemon rind grated

In the top of a double boiler, beat the egg yolks with salt until very thick and light colored. Stir in the sugar, and set the pan over hot (NOT boiling) water. Continue to beat steadily with the hand mixer until foamy (10-15 minutes). Add sherry and lemon rind, beat 1-2 minutes to blend well. Remove from the heat, cover and chill.

Apportion over drained pears in serving dishes. You can use the syrup to poach unripe peaches for tomorrow, or pour it over a ham slice to bake, if you like.

POIRES AU CHOCOLAT—for 6

6 pears, peeled, halved and cored
1 C apricot jam
1 lemon—grated rind and juice
¾ C water
¾ C minced candied fruits

¼ C Cognac
6 oz dark sweet chocolate bits

Combine jam, lemon and water, stirring over low heat into a thick syrup. Add the pears, and simmer covered for 30 minutes, turning occasionally until tender. Cool in the syrup.

Soak candied fruits in Cognac, while poaching the pears. When cooled, remove pears to a baking dish and fill the center cavities with the brandied fruit. Add chocolate to the jam sauce and reheat gently 15-20 minutes over low heat to melt the chocolate. Pour gently around the base of the pears. Cover the dish and leave at room temperature, basting occasionally with the chocolate sauce. Serve at room temperature with a little soft vanilla ice cream.

VARIATION: You can do this also with tart cooking apples. Peel, halve and core 1 apple per serving; poach in the jam syrup, but watch 'em—apples will cook more quickly than the pears. Follow directions through pouring chocolate sauce around the base of the apples, but use an oven-proof dish! Make a meringue of 3 egg whites with 8 T sugar (see METHODS). Spread over the apples, sprinkle with 2 T light-brown sugar, and brown for 5-6 minutes in a 350 oven. Serve either hot from the oven, or cooled to room temperature.

BORDELAISE PEACHES—for 4

4 *large* ripe peaches, peeled, pitted and halved
¼ C powdered sugar
1¼ C red Bordeaux
½ C sugar
2″ cinnamon stick

Cover the peaches with powdered sugar, and chill 1 hour or a bit more. Combine everything else and boil 1 minute; add the peaches with all their juice, reduce to a simmer and cook tender for about 10 minutes. Remove to a serving dish, and reduce the syrup over high heat for 5 minutes. Pour over the peaches, cover and chill.

MOCHA MOUSSE—for 6

> 10 T VERY strong coffee extract
> ½ lb bittersweet chocolate
> 3 C heavy cream
> ½ C powdered sugar
> ½ C Crème de Cacao
> Macaroon crumbs, if available

It is possible to buy coffee extract—or you can dissolve 5 T good soluble coffee in 10 T hot water. Add to the chocolate, and melt over lowest heat, stirring. Cool.

Lightly whip 2 C of cream, add powdered sugar, and beat until cream is stiff, slowly adding the Crème de Cacao. Fold into the chocolate mixture, pour into a mold and freeze without stirring for 3-4 hours. At serving time, whip the remaining cup of heavy cream, and do NOT sweeten. Garnish the portions with dry macaroon crumbs, or present naked and unashamed.

PLUMS IN PORT—for 6

> 12 large red or green plums
> 1 quart water
> 1 C sugar
> ¾ C white Port

Dissolve sugar in water and wine, bring to a boil; reduce

sharply to a simmer, and add plums washed but unpeeled. Cook very gently 5-8 minutes until tender, but do not break the skins. Chill in the syrup, and serve with a dollop of sour cream on top.

POMEGRANATE SOUFFLÉ—for 4

> 2 T each: flour, sugar
> ½ C pomegranate juice (you need 2 pomegranates)
> 3 egg yolks
> 2 tsp soft butter
> 4 egg whites, beaten stiff

Roll the fruit on a hard surface to loosen the seeds inside, but don't break the skin. With a small sharp knife, pierce the tuft end, holding it pointed over a bowl: a pomegranate squirts like mad! Squeeze out the juice ruthlessly with your hands, and get the last drops by smashing the seeds in a sieve.

Mix flour, sugar and juice smooth, and stir over gentle heat until it turns into sauce (4-5 minutes). Remove from heat, add butter and stir to melt. Let it cool while you beat the egg whites. Add egg yolks unbeaten to the sauce, and blend them well. Finally fold in the egg whites. Butter a 1-quart soufflé dish, dust with sugar, pour in the pomegranate mixture and bake 35-40 minutes at 350.

Serve hot with a Zabaglione sauce, either hot or cold. You can use the one for Zabaglione pears, chilled or at room temperature.

RUM CAKE UNANIMOUS—for 8-10

> ¼ C currants
> ¼ C light rum
> 6 eggs, separated

1 scant tsp cream of tartar
¾ C sugar
1 tsp almond extract
1 C flour
1 tsp baking powder

Soak currants in rum for 20 minutes. Beat egg whites foamy with cream of tartar, add ¼ C sugar and beat to meringue (see METHODS). Beat egg yolks with remaining sugar and almond extract until thick. Add to them currants and rum, plus flour sifted with baking powder. Mix gently but thoroughly. Fold in the egg whites, and bake in a well-greased tube pan 40 minutes at 325. At 30 minutes, make the following syrup:

½ C each: sugar, light rum, water
1 tsp almond extract

Bring sugar and water to a rolling boil; remove from heat, add rum and almond extract.

As soon as the cake is done, turn out on a plate and instantly douse it with the warm syrup. Then let it cool completely.

For Frosting:

¼ C strong black coffee
½ C semisweet chocolate bits

Melt together smoothly, and spread the top of the cake; it's not meant to cover the sides—just spread for a small finish on the top. You can set in the fridge briefly to firm the chocolate, and serve small portions—but nearly everyone comes back for more if there is any.

LEMON MOUSSE—for 6-8

2 T gelatin
¼ C water
¾ C lemon juice
6 eggs, separated
1½ C sugar
Grated rind of 3 lemons

Soften gelatin in water, add to lemon juice and stir over hot water for 5-6 minutes until gelatin is completely dissolved. Remove from heat. Beat the egg yolks with half the sugar until they are very thick and light-colored, and combine with gelatin mixture. Make a meringue of the egg whites with remaining sugar and lemon rind (see METHODS), and fold into the yolks. Pour into a serving dish, and chill 3-4 hours.

NOTE: This is a very light-textured dessert to finalize a rather hearty dinner of roast beef or stuffed goose. You can substitute orange juice and rind for the lemon, if you like.

MAMA'S ICEBOX CAKE—for Thanksgiving or Christmas, 12 to 20

Privately known in the family as Deadly Nightshade; one ladyfinger width is usually all anyone can digest without psychedelic reactions during the night.

½ lb sweet butter
½ C confectioner's sugar
4 eggs, separated
½ C brandy or fruit-flavored liqueur
½ tsp vanilla
½ C chopped unsalted nuts: almonds, Brazils, filberts
¾ C candied fruits, coarse-cut
24 fresh ladyfingers, halved

1½ lb almond macaroons—stale enough for crumbs
2 C heavy cream

Start this two days ahead. Spread the macaroons at room temperature to get stale. Prepare the candied fruits—and try to avoid the syrupy fruitcake combinations. If possible, get a box of assorted glacé fruits from a good candy shop, and mince them yourself. Marinate the bits in brandy or liqueur overnight.

The day before you mean to use the dessert, cream butter and sugar, add beaten egg yolks, nuts, vanilla and fruits with liqueur. Mix well and fold in the egg whites beaten stiff. Crush the macaroons into medium-fine crumbs. Lightly grease a 9" springform pan and dust with sugar. Stand the ladyfingers around the side, like a parapet. Sprinkle macaroon crumbs on the bottom, and make alternate layers of the butter filling and crumbs, ending with crumbs on top. Cover the pan loosely with waxed paper and chill 24 hours in the refrigerator. At serving time, whip the heavy cream and pile (unsweetened) over the top. Remove the pan side, and cut in small wedges.

Frosted cakes are not on my agenda; they are either too sweet or too gooey. Even unfrosted cakes are dubious for dessert, aside from simple luncheons or Sunday-night suppers. They are principally useful as "refreshments" with nonalcoholic drinks after a bridge party or PTA lecture, but extremely necessary for contributions to things like the church Christmas party.

BLACK WALNUT SPONGE CAKE

>5 eggs, separated
>1½ T lemon juice
>1 tsp grated lemon rind
>¼ tsp salt
>1 C sugar
>½ C chopped black walnuts
>1 C sifted flour

Beat egg yolks very thick with lemon rind and juice.

Make a meringue of egg whites with salt and sugar (see METHODS). Add the black walnuts, fold in the flour, and finally fold in the egg yolks. Bake 1 hour at 325 in ungreased tube pan. Let cool a full hour before removing from pan.

SPICE CAKE

>1 C butter
>2¼ C sugar
>5 eggs
>3 C flour
>1 T cinnamon
>1 tsp nutmeg
>½ tsp each: cloves, mace
>½ lb currants
>1 C sour cream
>1 tsp soda

Cream butter and sugar; add eggs singly, beating well after each one. Add flour sifted with soda, all the spices, currants and sour cream. Bake in a greased tube pan, 55-60 minutes at 350.

ANISE BUTTER LOAF

1 C butter
1 C sugar
4 eggs, separated
2 tsp ground anise
2 C flour
1½ tsp baking powder
¼ tsp salt
½ C milk

Cream butter and sugar until fluffy; add 4 whole egg yolks and beat well. Add flour sifted with salt and baking powder, anise and milk. Stiff-beat the egg whites and fold in last. Bake in greased floured bread tin 1¼ hours at 350—but test carefully for "done."

MAHOGANY CAKE

2 C flour
1¾ tsp baking powder
1 square bitter chocolate
½ tsp salt
1 C milk
1 stick butter
1 C sugar
3 eggs, separated
1 tsp vanilla

Measure the flour; reserve ¼ C with 1¼ tsp baking powder. Add remaining baking powder to ½ C milk. Melt the chocolate in the other ½ C of milk, and cool.

Cream butter and sugar; add egg yolks one at a time, beating well. Add the chocolate, salt, vanilla, and mix. Add 1¾ C flour and milk with baking soda; beat vigorously.

Beat the egg whites stiff. Fold the reserved flour and baking powder into main mixture, and finish by folding in the egg whites. Pour into a greased, floured tube pan and bake 40-45 minutes at 350. Cool 10 minutes before removing from the pan.

SOUR CREAM CAKE

½ C butter
1 lb dark-brown sugar
2 eggs
1 tsp vanilla
2½ C sifted flour
1 tsp each: soda, salt
1 C sour cream
¼ C cocoa dissolved in ½ C boiling water

Cream butter and sugar thoroughly. Beat in 2 whole eggs one at a time, plus vanilla. Combine flour, soda, salt, and add alternately with sour cream, beating smooth. Add the cocoa last, and mix well. Bake in two greased loaf pans 25 minutes at 375; reduce heat to 325 and bake 25-30 minutes more. Turn off the heat, open the oven door, and leave the cake to dry out as it cools.

NUN'S CAKE

1 C butter
1½ C sugar
5 egg yolks
2 egg whites
1 tsp almond extract
3 C flour
2½ tsp baking powder

½ tsp each: salt, cinnamon
1 C milk
1 T caraway seeds

Cream butter and sugar. Beat whole egg yolks singly into mixture. Beat egg whites separately with almond extract until very soft peaks, add to main bowl and beat thoroughly. Sift dry ingredients and add alternately with milk and caraway seeds. Bake in greased floured tube pan, 40 minutes at 250; lower to 325 for 35 minutes.

LITTLE SPONGE CAKES

3 eggs, separated
1 C sugar
Juice of ½ lemon
Grated rind of a whole lemon
½ C flour

Beat egg yolks VERY light; add sugar, lemon juice and rind. Beat 3 solid minutes. Add the flour (½ C, no matter what you think!). Beat egg whites stiff and fold in. Spoon into unbuttered cupcake tins, filling no more than halfway. Bake about 45 minutes at 300. Remove from oven, invert and cool completely before loosening.

BROWNIE CAKES

5 egg whites
9 oz powdered sugar
2½ T cocoa
2 oz crushed almonds

Beat the egg whites very stiff. Combine other ingredients

and fold in. Drop by measuring tablespoons onto a greased sheet and bake 40 minutes at 300.

PISTACHIO FANCIES

2 C flour
1½ tsp baking powder
½ tsp salt
⅔ C butter
1 C sugar
1 egg
1 tsp vanilla
½ tsp almond extract
¼ C fine-chopped unsalted pistachio nuts

Sift together flour, baking powder and salt. Cream butter with sugar; add egg, vanilla and almond extract. Work in the flour and divide the dough in half.

To one portion, add nuts and 2-3 drops of green food coloring. Form into a roll 10″ long, wrap in waxed paper and chill. Form the uncolored dough into a rectangle 10 x 4½″; cover and also chill—1 hour.

Wrap the white rectangle carefully around the green roll, pressing together minutely to prevent air spaces. You wish to bond the white with the green center. Wrap again and chill overnight. Slice ⅛″ thick, set 2″ apart on ungreased sheets and bake 10 minutes at 375, or until very lightly gilded. Cool thoroughly.

To Decorate:

Melt 6 oz semisweet chocolate—and either dip each cookie to coat halfway, or paint one whole side of each cookie. Set in the fridge for 10-15 minutes, until chocolate hardens.

MANTECADITOS—3 dozen

1 C plus 2 T butter
½ tsp salt
1½ tsp anise (ground)
1½ tsp grated lemon rind
½ tsp vanilla
1¼ C sugar
2 eggs
2 C flour

Cream first 5 ingredients well, then cream with the sugar to blend thoroughly. Add eggs singly, beating to mix well. Work in the flour. The dough should be stiff enough to form 1" balls. Set 1½" apart on greased sheets. Bake 20-25 minutes at 350 until edges brown lightly.

NOTE: For this you need cookie sheets with sides—as for jelly rolls. Otherwise you will be surprised (and saddened) to discover that your neat little dough balls have suddenly flattened and run over the edges . . . down to the oven floor, requiring an unanticipated cleaning job! These are not the tidiest cookies in appearance, but they taste very good.

NUTMEG HERMITS—6½ dozen

2 C light-brown sugar
1 C butter
4 eggs
4 C flour
1 tsp soda
1½ tsp nutmeg
½ tsp salt
¼ C milk (maybe)
2 C raisins

1 C chopped nuts—unsalted, any kind, but walnuts
are nice

Cream butter with sugar, add eggs singly and beat after
each one. Add everything else but milk—stir thoroughly
and consider the consistency: if really too solid, use some of
the milk. I rarely need it. Drop by small spoonsful 1½" apart
on greased sheets. Bake 12-15 minutes at 375.

DIOS KIFLI

½ C sugar
1 C butter
1½ C flour
½ C ground walnuts
1 tsp vanilla

Cream butter and sugar thoroughly. Add everything else
and work into a smooth dough. Cover and chill about 30
minutes. Roll very thin between *lightly* floured waxed
paper and cut in 1½" squares. Hand-form these into tiny
crescents: flop diagonal corners to the center, press to overlap securely, and set the crescents belly-side down on a
greased sheet. Twist the end into a horn-shape. Bake 15
minutes at 400, remove and cool slightly; roll *at once* in
plenty of powdered sugar. Set aside on waxed paper to cool
entirely—and roll again in powdered sugar . . . better
allow almost a full box!

PHEBE'S CHOCOLATE BALLS

3 squares of bitter chocolate, melted
1 C Brazil nuts, shredded
¾ C butter

½ C sugar
½ tsp salt
1 T heavy cream
1 tsp vanilla
2 C flour
Granulated sugar for rolling

Cream butter and sugar very thoroughly, add all but flour and mix thoroughly. Work in the flour to make a stiff dough. Pinch off small pieces and hand-roll to tiny balls (no more than 1"). Roll these thoroughly in granulated sugar, set on an ungreased sheet and bake 12 minutes at 350.

SHORTBREAD TEACAKES

¼ C sugar
1 C butter
2 C flour
¼ tsp salt
¼ C brandy
3 hardcooked egg yolks
1 whole egg
3 T sugar mixed with 1 tsp cinnamon

Cream butter and sugar. Add flour, salt and brandy. Press the egg yolks through a fine sieve and work into the dough thoroughly. Wrap and chill it for 30 minutes. Roll thin between floured waxed paper, cut shapes to your fancy (I've an inherited lot of cookie cutters, very fancy indeed!). Transfer tenderly to an ungreased cookie sheet. Lightly beat the whole egg and paint each cookie. Dust with the mixed cinnamon and sugar. Bake 25-30 minutes at 350.

SHORTBREAD PIE

> 1 C butter
> ½ C powdered sugar
> 2 C flour
> 1 C (approximately) slivered unsalted nuts and candied fruits
> 2-3 T additional powdered sugar

Cream sugar and butter thoroughly. Work in 1½ C flour ruthlessly; add remaining flour and work in lightly with your hands. Line a greased 8" pie pan or small square cake pan—use your hands, and press the dough smoothly into place, working completely up the sides; if using the pie pan, work it onto the flange and crimp around the edge with a fork, as for a pie. With a fork or pastry wheel, prick neatly into small wedges from edge to center. Decorate lavishly with the nuts and fruits, dust with remaining sugar, and bake about 20 minutes at 375 until a very light gold at the edges. Cool, and cut apart into the marked sections.

NOTE: This is fairly rich—mark the sections no more than 1½" wide.

THIN ALMOND COOKIES

> 2½ C blanched almonds
> 4 egg yolks
> 1 C sugar
> 2 T flour
> ⅛ tsp almond extract

Be sure the almonds are thoroughly dried out! If you blanch your own, dry them on a towel and set in a 200 oven for 20-30 minutes, shaking occasionally. Grind 1½ C medium fine and dry out again for 10-15 minutes; if using commercial blanched almonds, also dry out after grinding.

Mix unbeaten egg yolks with sugar, stirring until completely combined. Add flour and almond extract, plus ground almonds. Shape into sausage rolls 1½" in diameter; flour your hands lightly and handroll to a foot or more. Wrap in waxed paper and chill overnight in the fridge.

To cook, slice the cookies VERY thin with a sharp knife. Set on greased baking sheets and garnish each circle with a split almond. Bake 10-12 minutes at 350—no more. They should be only a pale gold shade.

Oddments

This is the All-Else Department: some unusual recipes for brunch, lunch, Sunday supper or midnight parties after the theater, items for Christmas gifts at the tree-trimming party, or the Community House blackmail contributions for bazaars and dinners. I never know how to classify these things, but they are far too useful to be ignored. Where else, for instance, can you put . . .

BAKED PAPAYA—6 for lunch

> 3 ripe papayas
> 1 C each: cottage cheese, cream cheese
> 1 tsp curry powder
> 3 T minced drained chutney
> 2 T Sultana raisins
> ½ C fine-minced water chestnuts
> 2 T melted butter
> 2 T cinnamon-sugar

Halve and seed the papayas unpeeled. At room temperature, smoothly blend together the cheeses and work in everything else but the butter and cinnamon-sugar . . . these are dribbled and sprinkled atop when you have stuffed the papayas. Bake 15-20 minutes at 450, serve hot—and note that this is decidedly filling! Flank with mixed green salad Vinaigrette, lots of iced tea with fresh mint sprigs, and a lime sherbet for dessert.

RAKOTTPALACSINTA—4 for lunch or Sunday supper

    2 eggs
    2 T flour
    1 T heavy cream
    2 T milk
    1 pinch of salt
    Butter—and a 10″ skillet

Mix the components extremely smooth, without beating the eggs too much. The final texture should be the consistency of thick olive oil; no lumps! Out of this batter you are to create crêpes, using 2 tsp of butter to grease the hot pan for each one.

Melt the butter, tilt to coat the skillet, and when sizzling, add about 2-3 T of the batter—you want only enough to make a thin coating over the buttered bottom of the pan. Cook 1-2 minutes to brown, flop over with the pancake turner, and cook another minute. Remove to a warmed plate.

Bluntly, this one is a fuss—but once you get the hang of making the crêpes, you are prepared for everything from Fruits de Mer to Suzette.

Having made a dozen pancakes (more won't hurt if you've leftover batter), you now make our faithful old "sauce" (see METHODS).

2 T butter
2 T flour
1 C milk
4 oz grated Parmesan
2 egg yolks
1 tsp salt
½ tsp pepper
8 oz minced boiled ham

Combine butter, flour and milk, and get it smooth over low heat, stirring for about 10 minutes. Add cheese, salt and pepper; stir to blend well. Beat the egg yolks lightly, and thicken the sauce (see METHODS). When thoroughly unctuously thickened, stir in the minced ham. Cover and remove from heat.

½ lb chopped fresh mushrooms
2 T butter

Sauté these separately for 10 minutes, stirring over medium heat.

The Final Assembly:

You can do the mushrooms and ham-cheese sauce ahead of time, holding covered at room temperature, and merely warming slightly while you are making the crêpes—but results are better for the end product if you prepare the dish as soon as the crêpes are cooked. If you leave them in a stack, they are apt to stick together and tear disastrously when you get to the last step.

Grease a deep 10" casserole. Set a pancake on the bottom, top with ham-cheese; repeat a pancake, top with mushrooms. Continue the layers to end with a pancake. Spread the fillings rather thinly to use everything. Dot the top crêpe with bits of 2 T butter, and cover THICKLY with 1 pint of sour cream. Cover the casserole, and bake 25 minutes at 350. Serve hot, in quarters.

This *can* be used as a hot-table hors d'oeuvre for 8, but frankly I think it too hearty to be followed by a full dinner menu. I like it preceded by a thin cold soup, flanked with broiled onion and green salad, finished off with mocha mousse.

PIPÉRADE—4 for brunch

> 3 T olive oil
> ¾ C chopped seeded green pepper
> ½ C peeled yellow onion, chopped
> 1 peeled garlic clove, pressed
> 3 ripe tomatoes, peeled, seeded and chopped
> ¼ C chopped boiled ham
> 2 tsp salt
> ½ tsp pepper
> ¼ tsp each: basil, oregano
> 2 T melted butter
> 6 eggs, lightly beaten

Heat the olive oil, and sauté pepper, onion and garlic over low heat for 10 minutes until onion is limp without browning. Add tomatoes, ham and seasonings. Cover and simmer 30 minutes over very low heat. Finally add the melted butter and the eggs. Cook/stir over low heat until the eggs are set to your taste. You can add some minced black olives and/or 2 T grated sharp Cheddar along with the eggs, if you happen to have them.

NOTE: What this IS is a Spanish omelet made with scrambled eggs, but it's lots less trouble than folding an omelet! Furthermore, it's good for a luncheon party teamed with popovers and salad . . . or equally good for the after-poker-party midnight snack, when it goes with coffee and French fries (if your husband won).

STOCKHOLM SCRAMBLE—4 for brunch

6 eggs
1½ C milk
1½ tsp each: sugar, salt
3 T butter

Beat the eggs VERY thoroughly with sugar and salt; add the milk and mix gently. Melt butter in the top of a double boiler over *simmering* water. Pour in the eggs, and cook covered for about 15 minutes until firmed. Serve on buttered hot toast or toasted English muffins . . . but if you are lucky enough to have fresh ripe garden tomatoes: peel 1 or 2 big ones, cut ¾″ thick, and set a slice on the hot-hot buttered toast BEFORE covering with the eggs.

As with Pipérade, this also is presentable for a simple luncheon party or midnight snack.

CORN FRITTERS—4 for brunch

1 C corn kernels
2 eggs, beaten
½ tsp each: salt, pepper
2 C flour
1 tsp baking powder

Sift together flour, salt, pepper and baking powder. Add corn to beaten eggs, and gradually stir in dry ingredients to make a heavy batter. You may need a bit more flour to get the right thick consistency. Heat ½″ of vegetable oil in the skillet, and drop in the batter by tablespoonsful, keeping well apart in the pan or they stick together. Fry gently, turning to brown all sides over medium low heat for 15 minutes, and drain well. These go with Canadian bacon and maple syrup.

NOTE: This is also where you use those leftover clams from Clam Broth . . . as well as any mussels or steamers left from last night's fish dinner. You'd be surprised how good they can taste at brunch! For these, plain bacon strips and melted butter, of course.

Kidneys are highly debatable. Personally I love *rognons*; so do many of my friends, but others practically faint at the idea of innards. Nevertheless, kidneys can appear succulently for brunch, lunch, or midnight supper. The following are for pleasing your most intimate friends, whom you know will share your gustatory joy.

BRANDIED VEAL KIDNEYS—for 4-6 at lunch . . . 8 for brunch

> 4 whole veal kidneys
> 4 T butter
> ½ C brandy
> 1 T extra butter
> 1 tsp dry mustard
> ¼ C minced fresh chives
> Juice of ½ lemon

Soak the kidneys in cold water to cover for 30 minutes.

Drain, and remove any white membrane the butcher missed. Melt the 4 T butter and brown the kidneys over high heat, turning constantly to get all sides for 5-7 minutes. Transfer to a covered casserole for 15 minutes at 350 in the oven. Remove the kidneys and keep warm. To casserole juices, add brandy and reduce by half over high boiling heat. Add the other T of butter with mustard, and kidneys sliced ¾" thick. Heat through without boiling for about 3-4 minutes. Add chives and lemon juice, stir to mix well and serve—on hot waffles for brunch, or with a bit of rice for lunch.

NOTE: All depends on the size of the kidneys: occasionally one biggie will serve 2, even 3, people. On this you must use your judgment.

ROGNONS MADÈRE—for 6 at lunch . . . or 8 for brunch

3 large veal kidneys, soaked and thinly sliced (½")
¼ C flour
¼ lb butter
½ C each: Madeira, sour cream
½ tsp each: salt, pepper

Dust the sliced kidneys with flour mixed with salt and pepper. Melt the butter, and brown the kidney slices quickly over fairly high heat, turning constantly for 4-5 minutes, until all sides are seared and there is no appearance of redness. They must be seared, but not over-cooked. Remove kidney slices to a warm dish. Add wine to the pan, lower the heat drastically and slowly-slowly add the sour cream, stirring gently to prevent a curdle. You cannot be impatient—but if despite your best efforts it disintegrates, *n'importe*! It will still taste good. Add a bit more pepper (no salt!) heat without boiling, pour over the kidneys and serve at once . . . and as above, it goes with buttered toast or rice, mashed potato, or spoon bread, depending on which meal it is.

CASSEROLE KIDNEYS—4 for lunch

> 4 veal kidneys, soaked and drained
> 2 each: scraped carrots, peeled yellow onions, thin-sliced
> 3 sprigs fresh parsley
> ½ stalk celery, thin-sliced
> ½ tsp salt
> ¼ tsp pepper
> 1 bay leaf
> ½ C dry white wine
> 4 T butter
> 2 tsp flour

Set the vegetables and seasonings in a deep casserole. Arrange the whole kidneys on top, with 2 T butter cut in lumps. Bake uncovered 20 minutes at 350 until kidneys are lightly browned. Pour over the wine, cover and bake 30-35 minutes longer until tender. Remove them from the casserole and keep warm. To pot juices, add a *beurre manié* of flour mashed with remaining butter (see METHODS), and cook thick and smooth over low heat, stirring for about 10 minutes. Strain to discard vegetables, and pour over the kidneys.

I think this goes on vermicelli cooked al dente, with a side plate of broccoli or fat fresh asparagus Hollandaise, and (just possibly) tiny muffins made in cupcake-sized tins, so they'll get done at the same oven temperature as the kidney casserole.

Garnitures—these are the small accompaniments for soup, salad, or to decorate the buffet table.

CHEDDAR APPLES

 ½ lb grated sharp Cheddar
 Whole cloves, a few watercress leaves, paprika

 Mold the cheese into 1½" balls with your hands. Insert a clove at the bottom, stick another head-first at the top (if you see what I mean?) and add a watercress leaf to simulate an apple. Dust very lightly with paprika, and chill. Use to decorate any cold meat platter, set one on the side or top of mixed green salad Vinaigrette, or put them all on a small dish for drinks before dinner.

POPPY TOAST

 Trimmed white bread slices
 A box of poppy seeds
 Soft butter

 There is no way to be specific on proportions—it's very simple, takes minutes to do if you're in the mood. What you DO is to flatten the bread with a rolling pin, spread with butter, sprinkle with poppy seeds and either cut in quarters—or if you are REALLY feeling frisky—roll up the whole slice to fasten with a toothpick. Bake 10 minutes at 425 on a greased baking sheet, or until gilded. Serve warm with soup, chef's salad, or as a quick cocktail titbit.

 Observe the possibilities: instead of poppy seeds, you can have sesame or caraway. Or ruthlessly mash pressed garlic cloves into the butter—this is obviously for an *intimate* party, but goes marvelously with a midnight supper of Fondue Bourguignonne. You can also use a sprinkle of cheese, or any herb or spice that fits the main event.

 This is the sort of thing that is so simple you forget about it—but you don't need a recipe. Just remember this is how to do it.

DIABLOTINS (this is a *pâte à chou*)

> 1 C water
> ½ tsp salt
> ¾ stick butter, cut in small hunks
> 1 C flour
> 4 whole eggs

Follow directions under METHODS. You will end with about 2 C of *chou* paste, with which you can do all sorts of things—but for Diablotins, mix in ½ C grated sharp Cheddar. Heat ¼ C butter with 1 T olive oil, and drop the *chou* paste therein to sauté until puffy gold. Use the measuring ¼ tsp in your kitchen set; you want marble-sized puffs. Drain well.

These replace croutons in hot soup or Caesar salad. Use your head on how many you'll need today and tomorrow; for a smallish party, you can halve the basic recipe—or when you've got as many Diablotins as wanted, you can bake the rest of the *chou* paste on greased sheets for 15-20 minutes at 400 until gilded, to serve hot with cocktails. For this, use the measuring tablespoon, making the puffs *small* and tidy.

VARIATION—to 1 C of *chou* paste with cheese, add 2 T dry sherry and bake for hot cocktail puffs.

MUSHROOMS FLAMBÉ—4 at midnight after the opera —with champagne?

> 1 lb lovely fresh white mushrooms—caps only
> ¼ C butter
> 1 C dry sherry
> ¼ C brandy
> ½ C heavy cream (warmed off-stage in the kitchen, NOT boiled)

8 pieces of hot toast, lightly buttered
a dash of salt

Melt butter in the chafing dish, sauté mushroom caps over medium low flame, stirring for 3-4 minutes until lightly browned. Add the sherry, raise the flame and stir while the pan simmers violently until nearly all liquid is gone. Add the brandy, and flame the pan (see METHODS), shaking the mushrooms until flames die. Finally add the warmed cream, stir to amalgamate everything, and serve on the hot toast—which you should appoint someone to make while you are creating the masterpiece.

This is a dish to be done in full view of the guests, seated around the table with their eyes glistening and tongues hanging out. If it is a *very* cold night, or a *very* long opera like *Les Troyens,* you might have a small cup of hot consommé first, and possibly accompany the mushrooms with two very thin slices of baked Virginia (or Westphalian) ham. The salad should be Endive Vinaigrette and the ending should be do-it-yourself—meaning a bowl of nuts for guests to crack, or apples to peel and sandwich with a slice of cheese, or just an assortment of cheeses with crackers and French bread. LASHINGS of coffee, of course . . . .

CREOLE EGGS—4 for lunch or midnight supper

8 hardboiled eggs, sliced
1 peeled white onion, thin-sliced
1 peeled garlic clove, pressed
1 T minced parsley
½ fresh green pepper, seeded and chopped
½ C milk
1 tin condensed cream of celery soup
¾ C canned tomatoes, drained
2 T butter

¼ C bread crumbs
½ C grated Parmesan

Sauté onion, green pepper and garlic in butter for 5 minutes over medium-low heat, stirring until onion is limp without browning. Add everything else but eggs, crumbs and cheese, and stir to blend well over low heat for 10-15 minutes. Taste the sauce critically, you may want a bit more salt and pepper than was provided by the tinned soup.

Set a few tablespoons of sauce in the bottom of a buttered casserole, top with sliced eggs, and repeat until you end with a layer of sauce. Sprinkle with crumbs and cheese. Bake 20 minutes at 375.

Here's another versatile recipe, with the added bonus of preparation ahead. Do it in the morning, leave it covered at room temperature until time to bake. You can use cream of mushroom or cream of asparagus soup, if you like . . . you can add minced mushroom stems and/or a thin-sliced celery stalk to the sauté pan if you use cream of asparagus soup. You can double, even triple the recipe to make a very large casserole dish for the Eastern Star luncheon buffet; figure it will stretch to 20 portions when there are other dishes to go with.

CHINESE FRIED RICE—for 4-6

2 T vegetable oil
2 peeled yellow onions, coarse-chopped
2 C cold cooked rice
2 lightly beaten eggs
1 T soy sauce
½ tsp salt
½ C minced ANYTHING: cooked shrimp, chicken, meat slivers, unsalted nuts, leftover vegetables . . . what have you.

Heat the oil, and sauté onions until lightly browned over medium low heat. Add the rice, and stir gently to separate the lumps; cook 4-5 minutes, stirring until rice is warmed through. Combine beaten eggs, soy sauce and salt; pour over the rice, and stir briskly to distribute throughout the pan. Add the minced leftover, and stir again to mix well. Cook 5-8 minutes more, stirring over low heat, and serve.

Observe the usefulness of this recipe! It is an entrée for lunch . . . but superb for the buffet table accompaniment to almost any main entrée. All that is required is to cook the rice yesterday; results are unsatisfactory unless the rice is completely cold—although you *can* do the rice this morning and stick in the fridge to chill. For lunch, that "minced ANYTHING" can be whatever was left on the bones of Sunday's roast, or the dibs and dabs of vegetables leftover from last night's dinner . . . for a buffet, you will choose something to go with the main entrée: if that is to be meat or poultry, you might use minced shrimp or drained chopped clams with your rice, but chopped nuts, minced water chestnuts, a few sliced ripe olives . . . literally *anything* goes, and the more inventive you are, the better. You can even use bits of fresh fruits, provided they are firm enough to hold their shape.

SWEET-SOUR CHICKEN CHAFING DISH

   3 whole raw chicken breasts
   2 T each: dry sherry, cornstarch, flour, soy sauce
   6 T olive oil
   1 large peeled minced onion
   6 T sugar
   ¼ C soy sauce
   2 T Cognac
   ½ C pineapple juice
   2 T white vinegar

3 T tomato sauce
1½ T cornstarch

Cut the chicken breasts into fairly large bite-sized pieces—big enough to spear with a toothpick. Mix the 2 T each of sherry, cornstarch, flour and soy sauce until smooth. Therein coat the chicken pieces individually, draining off any excess. Set the oil in a large skillet, and stir/fry the chicken over high heat for 4 minutes. Add minced onion, and continue to stir/fry over high heat for another 2 minutes until chicken is lightly browned on all sides.

Combine the remaining ingredients, stirring the cornstarch smooth in some of the liquids, and pour over the chicken pan. Lower heat to a minimum, and simmer 8-10 minutes, stirring gently until thickened. Transfer to the chafing dish to keep warm, and flank with a box of toothpicks.

I generally use this for a special hot appetizer at a cocktail party, but it is a useful addition to the buffet dinner table (double the recipe). As is, it is good for a luncheon party of six to eight, served on crisp Chinese fried noodles, or even for after-the-bridge-party in late evening.

The older one grows, the less one bothers with *presents* for Christmas or birthdays. Still, there are people one thinks about at such moments, and a tiny remembrance gaily wrapped is a touching attention. Food specialties are particularly good, because they'll be eaten up and pose no problem of storage for the recipient. For Leonie, who prefers tea to coffee any time, I make . . .

SPICED TEA

12 cardamom seeds, slightly crushed
1½ tsp of a crushed cinnamon stick
1 T dried grated orange peel
8 crushed whole cloves
½ C loose tea leaves

Crush the spices with a rolling pin—they are to be crushed, not powdered. Mix with the orange peel and add to the tea leaves—for which you should use a good imported brand rather than opening up commercial tea bags. Pack in a screw-capped glass jar (which is why you saved those empty marmalade jars!), and label neatly "Spiced Tea—use 1 rounded tsp per cup, and brew 5-6 minutes."

CURRY POWDER—for *pukka sahibs*

#1: 1 T each: cloves, mustard seed, poppy seed
    2 T each: cardamom, nutmeg, fennel seeds, chili peppers
    4 T each: ginger, white peppercorns
    8 T each: cumin, coriander, turmeric

Grind everything to a fine powder, using a mortar. This takes elbow grease and patience, but you can grind a bit at a time. Mix well together, and store in a tight-capped jar.

#2: 1 T cayenne
    2 T each: cloves, Jamaican ginger
    ¼ C each: black pepper, cardamom, caraway, red chili powder
    ¾ C ground coriander
    1 C turmeric

As above, grind to a fine powder in a mortar. For both mixtures, you can start with commercially ground spices to shorten preparation time. Store in a tight-capped jar or tin.

GREEN TOMATO JAM

Proportions for this depend on how many green tomatoes you have, obviously. In my youth we had a summer garden, and occasionally the tomatoes "got ahead of us." Then we picked the extras and got out the jam jars.

Peel and chop the green tomatoes. Set in a suitable pot with a very little water, to prevent scorching. Cook tender over low heat, stirring fairly often, until the tomatoes are suitably mushed.

Measure your pulp. Add an equal amount of sugar, plus 1 thin-sliced lemon for every 3 C pulp. Return to low heat, and cook until thick. Stir occasionally to prevent sticking. It will take about an hour . . . maybe longer if you have a lot of green tomatoes.

Sterilize the jam jars: wash and set in a pot of cold water—bring just to a simmer-boil over low heat. Remove and drain the jelly glasses without wiping—turn them upside down on a towel. You do this just as the jam is about finishing, so our polluted air cannot contaminate your efforts.

When the jam is thick, remove from the fire and add (if you like) drained preserved ginger cut in small bits. Fill the jam jars, top with a thin coat of melted paraffin, and let everything cool. When the glasses are at room temperature, add a second coat of melted paraffin, and label the sides.

NOTE: There is no way to be more precise about proportions and timing—this is an old-fashioned recipe, but I assure you it is worth your concentration. You can put it in plain jelly glasses, to use at home or donate to the food booth at the school fair . . . or you can (in a junk shop, hailed with cries of joy) find odd little china pots that have lost their tops; these you will sterilize and fill for presents to favored friends.

PEACH CHUTNEY

½ C chopped peeled yellow onion
½ lb raisins
1 peeled garlic clove
4 lb peeled fresh peaches
⅔ C crystallized ginger
2 T mustard seed
2 T chili powder
1 T salt
1 quart white vinegar
1¼ lb dark brown sugar

Finely grind onion, raisins and garlic. Mix with all else and set over low heat, stirring occasionally. When it reaches a simmer-boil, hold it there for 1 hour, until brown and fairly thick. Pour into sterilized jam jars or small bottles, and cap tightly.

SPICED NUTS

2 C raw nutmeats
1 beaten egg white
¼ C sugar
2 tsp cinnamon
¼ tsp nutmeg
½ tsp cloves
1 dash each: salt, pepper

The nuts can be anything, including peanuts, or a mixture of all sorts. Coat them in the frothy-beaten egg white. Combine everything else, and roll the nuts in the spiced sugar. Set on a baking sheet and place in a 350 oven for 15-20 minutes, shaking or turning them occasionally to prevent burning, until lightly gilded.

DADDY'S 1-2-3 PUNCH—and watch it!

    1 quart rye whiskey
    2 quarts fresh lemon juice
    3 quarts fresh orange juice
    1 large bottle of club soda
    1 bottle of maraschino cherries, including juice

Combine everything in a punch bowl over a small block of ice, stirring well. Serves 14-16, using small glasses—and I do mean watch it! This sneaks up on your guests, because it tastes simply like fruit juice. Present ample supplies of bland-flavored canapés—and for this one it is better to have everything already spread, or the guests become too happy to dunk for themselves.

Sample
Menus

BREAKFAST

I find it hard to believe anyone needs a written menu for breakfast or brunch. Even for VIP weekend guests, these meals are primarily fruit, hot bread and coffee, plus leisurely enjoyment of something one hasn't time to serve when rushing for the 8:02. Fresh fruit in season is more festive than a glass of juice, and ripe mango slices or persimmons in cream are more interesting than a half grapefruit, for instance. Instead of plain buttered toast, you can have hot muffins or popovers with jam.

For waffles, pancakes or French toast, the fancy touch is in the choice of toppings. Honey, maple syrup, cinnamon-sugar, jelly—or sour cream used instead of melted butter. Put 2 tsp of caviar (red or black) in the center of the sour cream, or dribble over it 1 T of any of the following: bottled Melba sauce, Grenadine syrup, minced preserved ginger, minced chutney. Eggs are at your discretion: I don't eat them, because they are my one allergy—and I can't prop-

273

erly cook anything I don't eat. I won't know how it ought to taste. That explains the paucity of egg recipes in my books.

Breakfast and brunch are not really a moment for alcoholic flavorings, but something depends on what you did last night. Occasionally, guests may be grateful for a Bloody Mary, a Bullshot or Screwdriver. If this seems indicated, set out the components for them to fix their own "hair of the dog," and produce LOTS of hot black coffee to follow. Thirty minutes later will be time enough to present brunch, one course at a time, but if you'd scheduled eggs, have them as an omelet or scrambled. The sight of a poached egg Florentine is apt to be unnerving on mornings after.

Here are my suggestions (* indicates recipes in this book):

#1

Half a ripe papaya
*Pipérade with Bacon Strips
*Plain Hot Muffins, with choice of jam

#2

Baked Apples with cream
*Fresh Corn Fritters
Canadian Bacon
*Cousin Ida's Gems, with honey or jam

#3

Fresh Ripe Strawberries, with powdered sugar to dip
Waffles with Sour Cream and browned sausages
*Stockholm Scramble (serve alongside the waffle)

LUNCHEON

Luncheon menus depend upon the season: if hot weather, they must be light, but even in winter, luncheon should be restrained. One drink with a very simple appetizer is sufficient for a prelude. I rarely serve wine with luncheon; tea or coffee is better. Sometimes I have a table appetizer, but mostly I present an entrée with salad and a modest dessert. That's for women. If there are husbands, the menu should be more substantial.

#1

With drinks: *Chinese Sour Cream Dip, with raw vegetables
At table:
   *Canteloupe Soup
   *Parmesan Sole
   Brussels Sprouts with lemon butter
   Mixed Green Salad Vinaigrette, with tomato wedges
   Ice cream with liqueur sauce
NOTE: Lemon butter is simply 1 tsp grated fresh lemon rind in ¼ C melted butter. You can use 2 T of any liqueur for whatever flavor ice cream you like. Crème de Cacao is good with coffee ice cream.

#2

With drinks: *Buttered radishes
   *Foie de Volaille with crackers
At table:
   *Caviar Mushrooms
   *Cathy's Quiche aux Fruits de Mer

Endive Vinaigrette
*Frosted Grapes

This menu is good if there are men; they always like a spread to go with drinks.

#3

With drinks: *Walnut Spread with crackers
   *Céleri Ordinaire
At table:
   *Clam Broth
   *Pompano Charpentier
   French-Fried potatoes (if there are men)
   Buttered French-style beans (if there are NOT men)
   *Asperges Dijon
   *Mocha Mousse

DINNER

The *formal* dinner is not in the scope of this book. The last time I gave one was fifteen years ago, on behalf of my father, who wished to entertain a dozen very distinguished scientists congregating in Washington. They came from all over the world, which made for an interesting conversation as daddy didn't speak anything but English. They also all had wives—or said they did, although there were at least two whom my experienced eye instantly classified as "traveling companions."

The final tally was 26 people. It required three waitresses, our regular maid to supervise the kitchen, plus bribing her husband into a white jacket to open the door and hang up coats. It took me one week of unremitting toil to market and cook. It cost daddy four hundred dollars by the time we got through, but he WOULD do it, even if it killed all the rest of us. Need I say his work load was limited to ordering the wine? I still have that menu:

With pre-dinner drinks:
    Pâte à chou farcis variés
    Oeufs durs farcis Brasileira
    Canapés Chauds (fromage)
    Canapés Froids (Pâté de foie, jambon persillé)
At table:
    Consommé Double, garni Diablotins
    Fruits de Mer, sauce Nantua
    Suprêmes de Volaille Champagne
    Petits Pois Française
    Pommes de terre Anna
    Salade d'endives vinaigrette
    Petits Babas au Rhum, Flambé
    Café, Liqueurs de choix

I even typed it out neatly on individual place cards in French. Every now and then I see that sheet in my binder and shudder in memory, although it went off very well. Both the professors with traveling companions kissed me *passionately* behind the swinging door to the kitchen—which is probably as close as I shall ever come to a Nobel Prize. Everybody else kissed me on both cheeks, except the Russians, who merely shook hands— vigorously.

The next year that Congress was in Stockholm, thank heavens.

Actually some of those recipes are in this book. *Oeufs durs farcis Brasileira* is #4 under Stuffed Eggs; *Canapés Chauds* is translated here as Cheese Canapés, and the *Suprêmes de Volaille* is just Chicken Breasts in Champagne. The *Pâte à Chou Farcis Variés* is the same as the recipe here for Diablotins—minus the cheese in the basic paste; that is, I baked them plain, and they were then stuffed with a teaspoon each of creamed or minced this-and- that . . . mushrooms and curried sautéed ground beef—but I think there was a crab one, too. (Make the puffs any time; stuff an hour before serving, and reheat 6 minutes in a 350 oven.)

You'll find a recipe for *Pommes de Terre Anna* in any standard cookbook, and by now you know how to make Vinaigrette (I told you myself in the introduction to Salads). *Petits Pois Française* is only sufficient boxes of frozen "tiny peas" for the crowd, steamed with thin shavings of peeled white onion—allow 1 onion per box. I will agree that the other items are a fuss, but you do see how it is possible to present apparently fancy dishes fairly easily?

However, the menus that follow are geared to the realities of today's world—of which the most pressing is: WHO washes up? My parties are scheduled for the night before the maid comes. I am honorable enough to warn her of KP. I scrape and rinse plates, leave pots soaking. If you don't, your slavey will develop a misery and fail to show.

For the sit-down dinner, my personal menu book produces:

#1

With drinks: *Clam/Crab Dip with raw vegetables
  *Roquefort Normande with crackers
At table:
  *Frigid Eggs with torrid Sauce
  *Beef Wellington
  Fresh buttered peas with sliced water chestnuts
  *Hearts of Palm Vinaigrette
  *Rum Cake Unanimous

#2

With drinks:
  *Shrimp Dip
  *Anonymous Cheese Puffs
At table:
  Snails
  *Squab Oporto
  *Shredded Carrots
  *Potatoes Catalan
  Mixed Green Salad with *Avocado Dressing
  *Zabaglione Pears

#3

With drinks:*Broiled Water Chestnuts
  *Pâté Casanova
At table:
  *Breadfruit Vichysoisse
  *Poulet à l'Ail
  *Artichokes Granadina
  Sliced tomatoes on watercress, *Cucumber dressing
  *Bordelaise Peaches

THE COCKTAIL PARTY

For the cocktail party, if you MUST give one, the larger the crowd the more variety you need, and dietary restrictions are less important. Inevitably there will simply BE something for everyone. The small party should still loosely adhere to "1 with meat, 1 without" plus vegetables for dipping, and perhaps a hot cheese titbit to offer when the party is in full swing.

I prefer to concentrate on ample supplies of a few dishes at the party of twelve to twenty—because everybody can *see* what's to eat and think you are pretty cheap (or a lousy housekeeper) if there's not enough of each dish to go all the way round. The more guests you have, the less they notice when an empty plate or dunk dish is quietly removed —particularly if you set several feeding stations strategically about your rooms. It is also easier on you to make double or triple of one recipe than to be riding rapidly in all directions with a dozen different items. Choose among the dips and dunks under Appetizers, and limit the impressive titbits to one for 8-10 people, two for 10-20, and three for more than twenty. All should be things that take the least amount of last minute attention, unless you have an assistant in the kitchen . . . but for more than ten guests, appoint a friend to help in carting the hot goodie around.

For example:

Clam/Crab dip

Janice's chopped liver

A Cheese Ball

Stuffed Eggs

Chicken Calicut

With this one, almost everything is done yesterday, leaving only the eggs to be stuffed this morning—no matter how carefully you wrap, they never look *quite* so appetizing if they were held overnight. Today also you prepare the raw vegetables to accompany the dip, and arrange the plates of crackers. If you did the chicken in advance, you have only to hot it up gently and transfer to the chafing dish to keep warm while you get dressed for the party. The final last touch is to stir in the toasted coconut while you wait for the first arrivals. Leave it and the eggs in the kitchen though! Let the guests begin with dip, pâté and cheese. *Then* you produce the chafing dish to sit in a central spot, and trot the eggs from one person to another. I allow one egg per person with a few extra for good measure. If there are any leftover, it's curried eggs for tomorrow night's dinner.

Thus, the *theory* of the cocktail party is to start the guests with do-ahead dips and spreads and present the specialty when everyone will notice it—not merely to enhance the party, but also to be sure nobody drinks without eating! Conversely, the buffet dinner need not present any specialty with the drinks, because there are plenty of dishes to come. While you want the guests to eat something, you do not wish them to be so full they are unable to appreciate the glories of the buffet table. Here is a menu for 16 people:

Shrimp dip *and* Curry dip, with raw vegetables

Pâté Allemande, with crackers and party rye slices

A cheese board—IF there's a reliable cheese shop from which to make an assortment: Edam, Chiberta, Port Salut, *ripe* Camembert and Brie. Otherwise, the Liqueur Cheese Pot and Fromage Hindu.

BUFFET

For the buffet table itself, using double recipes:

Loong Ha Peen

Pork Taiwan

Pignon Pilau

Buffet Spinach

Jellied Guacamole with Cucumber Dressing

Céleri Rémoulade

Mixed fruits in wine

In this line-up, the dips, pâté, celery, guacamole and fruit dessert can be done yesterday. This morning you do the Pork Taiwan nearly to completion and hold at room temperature for the final few moments needed to heat for serving. Similarly you do the spinach and hold at room temperature; it will take a few minutes under the broiler to finish.

Finally you organize all components for Loong Ha Peen, and measure out the rice for the pilau. The end cooking will take about half an hour to get everything to the buffet—and while the guests are having their second drink, you will not be missed.

One thing: this particular menu does not entirely follow the rules. If your party is on Friday, you had better add an egg dish—just in case. Curried eggs will go nicely with the pilau, or you can have Creole Eggs.

Something else I haven't specifically stated is that all parties, particularly buffets, can incorporate commercial ready-to-serve items—if you happen to possess a local tradesman for some specialty. In general, the frozen cocktail puffs will be far too expensive for a large party, but I often use one package for four to six guests, flanked with my own dip or spread. There also exist gourmet cheese balls in a package, and assorted frozen canapés. I am always adventurous about trying something new (if it doesn't cost too much), but I've learned an interesting thing: all the processors are constantly putting out new items, . . but these are never market-tested in New York or any other large city!

In fact, the first thing I do when visiting in any suburban or rural area is to visit the supermarket. I always find a number of goodies, but unless they ring the bell in suburbia, they never reach D'Agostino.

Similarly, there may be a marvelous little shop in your neighborhood that makes a delicious coffee cake, or a delicatessen with a special touch for potato salad. Annually, when I spend Christmas in Chevy Chase, my bachelor brother pays off all arrears of hospitality by an evening party "Nine p.m.—*until* . . ." Occasionally there are still a few guests for 6 a.m. breakfast—they have consumed three pots of coffee and are seriously discussing the newest developments in solid state cyclotrons (or something) while listening to Mahler.

But for the basis of our party, we make use of the local specialists. There are 2" egg rolls from a Chinese restaurant; they bear no relation to the frozen packaged varieties. There is sashimi from a Japanese restaurant; they throw in the shredded horseradish, but my brother makes the wasabi powder sauce. At this point, we are already well advanced on a menu for forty people: Chinese mustard, Duck Sauce, Plum Sauce, and plenty of toothpicks are all we need.

The rest is up to me. I present Tikia, Cha Sui (which uses the same sauces as the egg rolls), a large bowl of ice upon which cuddle several pounds of cooked cleaned shrimp (with a bowl of Whiskey Sauce for dipping), a small tinned ham baked with honey and chilled—or perhaps a handsome cold boiled tongue (which my brother loathes; he can NEVER believe it was practically all eaten during the evening!). Sometimes I have Sweet-Sour Chicken Chafing Dish, or cocktail franks with a mustard sauce—not everything every year, you understand.

For this sort of party, one does not need vegetables or salads—the guests (presumably) ate dinner at home three hours ago . . . although I sometimes wonder. We use paper plates and plastic forks or toothpicks. There is coffee, but no dessert. There are also lots of bits and pieces set about: salted nuts, bowls of black and green olives, a large dish of chicken liver pâté with crackers in the living room, a tray of deviled breadsticks (sorry, that was in *Simple Gourmet Cookery*), and perhaps Crab Dunk with raw celery sitting atop the TV set.

The liquor flows freely, but wherever you go that evening there will be something to nibble. Nobody, but NOBODY will have an auto accident on the way home.

Observe the simplicity of this: *every* item is done beforehand. The egg rolls sit in the electric frying pan turned to Warm; Tikia sits in a second pan atop an electric hot plate also turned to Warm. All else is cold. I merely set it forth, and join the party with an easy mind. I do not even trot about with a specialty, for this sort of party it is not needed.

Admittedly, you may not have a Tom's Kitchen for egg rolls, or a place to procure sashimi (although you *can* do this yourself: it requires a slab of *fresh* tuna and a razor-sharp knife with which to slice thinly on the bias as for London Broil), but look thoughtfully at the local shops. You might find a delicatessen who makes *small* stuffed cabbage rolls, and there exist tinned Swedish meatballs (köttbuller) that could be served in your own sauce.

I said in the beginning that a menu must be what you like to prepare and what your guests will like to eat. Thus these menus are merely suggestions to use as a springboard for creating your own.

Alphabetical
Index

285

Poires au chocolat, 238-239
Pomegranate soufflé, 241
Zabaglione pears, 237-238

EGGS
Arabian, 75
Creole, 265
Dip, 44
Pipérade, 258-259
Stockholm scramble, 259
Stuffed (5), 48-49

FISH
Buffet shrimp, 124-125
Cathy's quiche aux fruits de mer, 115
Clams in wine sauce
Cod in sour cream, 114
Crabmeat casserole, 123
Fillets farcis, 113-114
Henri's crab casserole, 123-124
Leonie's lobster Newburgh, 120-121
L'Homard à deux, 121
Lobster pernod, 121-122
Loong Ha Peen, 125-126
Paprika shrimp, 119
Parmesan sole, 112-113
Pompano Charpentier, 112
Shrimp:
    Basquais, 118-119
    Brandado, 117-118
    Cold curry, 119-120
    with Eggplant, 116-117
    on the Half Shell, 115-116
    Obregon, 116

GARNITURES
Cheddar apples, 262-263
Diablotins, 264
Poppy seed toast, 263
Green Tomato Jam, 270-271

LAMB
Agnello con limone, 154
Gigot en croute, with variation, 152-154
Marsala lamb shanks, 151-152

MEAT
Agnello con limone, 154
Bohemian veal, 159-160
Boeuf Bourguignonne, 149-150
Beef Wellington, 144-146
Casserole kidneys, 262
Chu Jou Cheju-Do, 156-157
Côtelette de veau foyot, 161-162

Filet severine, 147-148
Flank steak orientale, 149
Fondue Bacchus, 146-147
Gigot en croute, with variation, 152-154
Marsala lamb shanks, 151-152
Porc aux fruits, 157
Pork Taiwan, 155-156
Rognons madère, 261
Roquefort steak, 148
Rum loin, 155
Sour cream chops, 157-158
Veal in aspic, 161
Veal birds, 162-163
    Flambé, 163-164
Veal kidneys, brandied, 260-261
Veau à la gendarme, 158-159
Veau à l'orange, 160
Papaya, Baked, 255
Peach Chutney, 271

PORK
Chu Jou Cheju-Do, 156-157
Porc aux fruits, 157
Pork Taiwan, 155-156
Rum loin, 155
Sour cream chops, 157-158
Rakottpalacsinta, 256-258

SALADS
Accompaniment shrimp, 223
Avocado mold, 226
Buffet vegetable, 227-228
Céleri rémoulade, 70-71
Chicken for lunch, 223
Chicken orientale, 224-225
Dressings:
    Avocado (3), 218-219
    Caviar mayonnaise, 218
    Chutney, 217
    City club, 217
    Coleslaw, 219-220
    Cucumber, 216
    For shrimp and watercress, 220
    Mayonnaise Dijon, 216-217
    Vinaigrette, 215
Feodor, 221-222
Garbanzos chillenos, 221
Garbanzos tout-simple, 71
Jellied guacamole, 225
Lettuce, stuffed, 226
Praha coleslaw, 231-232
Raw mushroom, 222
Shellfish fancy, 229-231
Shrimp Elspeth, 229